PAPER CHASE

PAPER CHASE

PAPER CHASE

PAPER CHASE

By Sheila "Honey" Reed

Repairing The Bridge

Maricopa, Arizona

PAPER CHASE

PAPER CHASE

Published by:

Repairing The Bridge

Maricopa, AZ 85138

Email: Sheilareed@repairingthebridgeaz.com

Sheila "Honey" Reed, Publisher

ALL RIGHTS RESERVED

No part of this book may be reproduced or transmitted in any form or by any means—electronic or mechanical, including photocopying, recording, or by any information storage and retrieval system—without written permission from the authors, except for the inclusion of brief quotations in a review.

Books are available at exclusive discounts for bulk purchases, sales promotions, fundraising, or educational purposes.

Copyright © 2017 by Sheila "Honey" Reed

PAPER CHASE

ISBN #: 978-0-692-05232-7

Library of Congress Control:2018938808

PAPER CHASE

DEDICATION

For my Sister:

Thank you for believing in me and praying for me. I was blessed to be in the presence of an Angel for a short time. When everyone, including myself, said "I could not". You reminded me, "I could do all things through Christ who strengthens me. Sister, our connection has always amazed me. We often knew what each other's thoughts were, without saying one word. The depth of your love, smile, and faith will forever be etched in my heart. I will miss you forever! Until we meet again!

PAPER CHASE

ACKNOWLEDGEMENTS

Thank you, Jesus, for each experience and each life lesson, good and bad; for without them, I would not be me. Thank you, Jesus, that there is a blessing in every lesson. Thank you, Ellen Michelle (Cuz)! You were instrumental in the completion of this book. Thanks for your encouragement, effort, and feedback. Let's get it!

PAPER CHASE

Table of Contents

Journey to Resilience: Overcoming, Healing, and Self-Discovery

Preface

Poem: Sitting on the Sidelines

1. Chapter One: The Beginning - Page 1

2. Chapter Two: Unraveling Threads - Page 3

3. Chapter Three: Secrets and Lies - Page 8

4. Chapter Four: The Breaking Point - Page 13

5. Chapter Five: A New Direction - Page 33

6. Chapter Six: The Unexpected Visitor - Page 43

7. Chapter Seven: Confrontation - Page 49

8. Chapter Eight: Searching for Answers - Page 61

9. Chapter Nine: The Road Less Traveled - Page 77

10. Chapter Ten: Lessons in the Shadows – Recognizing Abuse - Page 98

PAPER CHASE

11. Chapter Eleven: The Cost of Loyalty - Page 120

12. Chapter Twelve: Breaking the Silence – Finding My Voice - Page 141

13. Chapter Thirteen: Embracing Solitude and Self-Worth - Page 154

14. Chapter Fourteen: Setting Boundaries, Reclaiming Power - Page 178

15. Chapter Fifteen: The Power of Resilience - Page 196

16. Chapter Sixteen: Sharing the Story – Inspiring Change - Page 220

17. Chapter Seventeen: Building a Life of Meaning - Page 226

18. Epilogue: Triumph and Transformation - Page 237

Resources for Healing - Page 247

Questions for Reflection - Page 267

Where Are They Now - Page 274

PAPER CHASE

About the author - Page 284

PAPER CHASE

PREFACE

Overcoming abuse while still experiencing it is an extremely tough challenge. Many times, we feel broken and confused by the effects of abuse. Abuse can show up in different ways, such as addiction, depression, anxiety, Post Traumatic Stress Disorder, dissociation, and various other mental health disorders. Pursuing what matters in life and aligning with our values, which are often intangible, will help us make smart decisions about our circumstances. We can then learn to navigate life's challenges and ultimately reach our destined success. I hope this story helps you understand and overcome your own struggles.

Ask yourself: "What do we do when we take the wrong road on our life journey, and how can we reach our destiny? What happens when we don't know how to value ourselves enough to change circumstances that are detrimental to our well-being?"

PAPER CHASE

In Stacey Carson's world, financial stability, loyalty, and independence are the defining characteristics of success. Stacey always dreamed of a perfect life—happily married with children, owning a house, having a dog, and driving two cars—by any means necessary. But what price would she pay to attain what she considered success?

Stacey found herself in a challenging cycle where many of the men she encountered betrayed or mistreated her. Yet, amidst this turmoil, she began to recognize that her past experiences shaped her understanding of relationships. Despite achieving financial stability, she learned that true success includes a sense of safety and emotional well-being. The wounds of betrayal, while deep, became catalysts for growth and self-discovery. Though she initially struggled with trust, shame, and regret, Stacey's journey led her to seek love in healthier ways. Embracing solitude allowed her to heal, and in her pursuit of success, she gradually learned to value herself more. Her life transformed from one of tragedy and pain to one of resilience and hope. By setting boundaries that required respect from herself and others, Stacey embarked on a powerful healing journey that inspired joy and tears of triumph.

PAPER CHASE

Time Spent

As I sit on the sidelines, feeling hopeless and powerless in the name of love, I wish I could call some plays or even take him out of the game.

Oh, how I wish I could save her from defeat, disappointment, mistreatment, unhappy days, and shame. I long to show her that it's better to love ourselves instead of depending on someone else for love. Please, God, show me how to help her avoid pain and teach her that our spirits were meant to be as free as a dove.

I wish I could protect her from those she loves—her mother, her children, and her friends—who turn their backs on her because they don't understand why she stays.

Oh, how I wish I could save her from the loneliness that will come while she hopes for a better day. The time we waste praying for better

PAPER CHASE

times can never be reclaimed. Wake up! Pay attention! When all the time is spent, and the truth is revealed, the regret we feel will not lessen the sting of time lost, nor will apologies or positive thinking. The time is gone!

I wish I could save her from all the tears and heartache that false hope brings. But I cannot save her from her choice of destruction or the commitment she feels represented by those rings.

In the end, she will come to realize, just like we all eventually do, that it is better to heed the warning signs that life teaches us, rather than feeling defeated.

While the time may be lost forever, the experience can empower us to change someone else's destiny by sharing how we overcame the cycle of abuse and teaching others to love themselves better than we did. Now, we must decide before it's too late: do we run now or later?

PAPER CHASE

Well, in case you are wondering, "her" was me... Run now! Too much time has already been spent!

PAPER CHASE

PAPER CHASE

CHAPTER ONE

Every journey begins with a single step, and often, it's the courage to take that step that defines our path. Life will throw challenges along the journey, but each obstacle is an opportunity for growth. Just like Stacey in her story, we can confront our past, learn from it, and reshape our futures.

Remember, no matter how heavy the burden we carry, love—especially self-love—can be our guiding light. It is crucial to recognize our worth and embrace the power we must change our circumstances. Surround yourself with those who uplift and inspire you, and don't be afraid to set boundaries with those who don't.

As we reflect on our experiences, let's commit to breaking the cycles that hold us back. Each choice we make, whether to step forward or to

PAPER CHASE

retreat, shapes not just our own destiny but also the lives of those around us.

So, let's take a moment to appreciate the strength we have within us. Let's choose to love ourselves fiercely and advocate for our own happiness. The journey might be tough, but it's worth it. Let's share our stories, support one another, and inspire each other to rise above, knowing that brighter days are ahead.

You have the power to rewrite your story; make it one of resilience, hope, and unyielding love. Keep moving forward; your best days are yet to come!

PAPER CHASE

CHAPTER TWO

I was ten years old when my mother sent me to live with my grandmother. Big Momma's house was different—different in a bad and scary way! My Big Momma was working even more, and my great-grandmother was very ill. Strange things were happening around the house. The smoke carried odd smells that seemed to turn my uncles and Auntie June into zombies. Something wasn't right, I thought. I told myself I wasn't scared and that I had to be strong to help Big Momma care for Grandma Henrietta, but I was terrified to even walk down the long hallway that led to my great-grandmother's room.

The "monsters" began to visit again, night after night, while I was sleeping. I started to stand up for myself and say, "NO, NO more!" This often resulted in being overtaken by force. The fighting excited the monsters. My ten-year-old body would feel sore from struggling with them. The only way to

PAPER CHASE

keep them from coming for me was to sleep in the room with my great-grandmother.

This horrifying experience had been going on since I was five! Where on earth was my protector? I wondered why Auntie June was never around. What was happening here? I heard Big Momma talking to God, asking Him to heal her mother. She was troubled by diabetes that was violently taking my grandmother's limbs. I wanted to tell her what was going on, but I feared she would blame me, just like the monsters said she would.

One morning, when I went in to wake Grandma Henrietta, she didn't wake up. She looked like a peaceful Agelique. I remember she was wearing a light pink gown, and her silky, fine hair was pulled back into a ponytail. My grandma died that year from complications of diabetes. There was still no sign of my protector: my grandpa. Auntie June was pregnant again with her second child and was hardly around. I helped Big Momma take care of the house and soon delivered fish dinners on my bicycle. One day, just like years earlier, my grandpa

PAPER CHASE

suddenly appeared. It turned out that the time he spent marching in prison had led to a mental illness. He had been at a state mental hospital. It didn't matter how crazy anyone thought he was; he loved me and wasn't about to let anyone hurt me. Finally, I would be protected.

Sharon came back into my life. She was living with a slick-talking guy named Curtis from the Midwest, who looked old enough to be her father. It turned out that Curtis was fifteen years older than my mom, who was in her mid-twenties. He was mean, and I didn't like him. But for some reason, Stephanie, my little sister, loved him and seemed to be his favorite. When I visited their house, my mom was always crying and covered in bruises that she hid under makeup. Thinking back, Big Momma must have suspected abuse because whenever I returned to my mother's house, she would question me about what was going on. If Curtis was hurting Sharon, Big Momma vowed to take him out with the pistol she kept in her purse. I overheard Big Momma praying to God, asking Him to please protect Sharon.

PAPER CHASE

One night when I stayed over at Sharon's, I was awakened by loud banging and screaming. Sharon ran into the room where Stephanie and I were sleeping, completely naked, with Curtis close on her heels. She jumped into a recliner in the corner. Just then, I heard a noise that sounded like metal snapping together. Curtis had cocked his shotgun and pointed it at Sharon. I quickly jumped in front of my mom and yelled, "Nooooooo, you can't kill my mom!" Curtis hit me with the shotgun, and the next thing I knew, I was waking up with a terrible headache in my grandmother's bed. She was sitting on the side of the bed, praying, tears rolling down her face. "Lord, you said you would break the chains... "Lord, you said she would be great... protect her, Lord!" she shouted.

By now, I was pretty fed up with all this talking to a God who wasn't answering. I continued to live with Big Momma, but she was getting very ill from diabetes. My grandpa was still in and out of the state hospital with mental issues. The family was a mess, filled with constant arguing and illegal activity; the siblings were often at each other's throats. Everyone seemed to either be fighting, acting like zombies, or in jail. The only time we felt somewhat normal was when we would go over to Aunt Laura's after church (Big Momma's sister).

Aunt Laura was married to a kind Creole man named Reverend Cooks, who baptized me. I never knew his first name; even Aunt Laura called him Reverend Cooks. Aunt Laura had adopted two children because she could not have children of her own. Later, I heard some family members say that she had been raped at a young age, which left her unable to conceive. I think her two children must have had twenty kids apiece—there were so many of them, and none had dads either. All the cousins made Sundays even better because I had a lot of kids to hang out with. Aunt Laura had a farm with the meanest chickens in the world and geese that would chase you, boy, it stunk in that yard!

PAPER CHASE

CHAPTER THREE

One day, just like years before, my grandpa suddenly reappeared. It turned out that the marching he had done in prison had led to a mental illness, and he had been staying in a state mental hospital. It didn't matter how crazy anyone thought he was; he loved me and wasn't about to let anyone hurt me. Now I would finally have protection.

Sharon came back into my life. She was living with a slick-talking guy named Curtis from the Midwest, who looked old enough to be her father. It turned out that Curtis was fifteen years older than my mom, who was in her mid-twenties. He was mean, and I didn't like him. But for some reason, my little sister Stephanie loved him and seemed to be his favorite. When I visited their house, my mom was always crying and had many bruises that she covered with makeup. Thinking back, Big Momma must have suspected abuse because whenever I returned to my mother's house, she would question me about what was going on. If Curtis was hurting Sharon, Big Momma vowed to take him out with the pistol she kept in her purse. I overheard her praying to God, asking Him to please protect Sharon.

One night, while I stayed over at Sharon's, I was awakened by loud banging and screaming. Sharon ran into the room where Stephanie and I were sleeping; she was buck-naked with Curtis close behind her. She jumped into a recliner in the corner. Just then, I heard a noise that sounded like metal snapping together. Curtis had cocked his shotgun and pointed it at Sharon. I quickly jumped in front of her and yelled, "No! You can't kill my mom!" Curtis hit me with the shotgun, and the next thing I knew, I was waking up with a terrible headache in my grandmother's bed. She was sitting on the side of the bed praying, tears rolling down her face. "Lord, you said you would break the chains... Lord, you said she would be great... protect her, Lord!" she shouted.

PAPER CHASE

By now, I was pretty sick of all this talking to a God who wasn't answering. I continued to live with Big Momma, but she was getting very ill from diabetes. My grandpa was still in and out of the state hospital with mental health issues. The family was a mess, filled with constant arguing and illegal activity; the siblings were nearly arch enemies. Everyone seemed either to be fighting, acting like zombies, or in jail. The only time we appeared normal was when we would go over to Aunt Laura's after church (Big Momma's sister).

Aunt Laura was married to a kind Creole man named Reverend Cooks, who baptized me. I never knew his first name; even Aunt Laura called him Reverend Cooks. Aunt Laura had adopted two children because she could not have children of her own. Later, I found out that she had been raped at a young age, which left her unable to conceive. I think her two children must have had twenty kids apiece—there were so many of them, and none had fathers either. All the cousins made Sundays even better because I had lots of kids to hang out with.

PAPER CHASE

Aunt Laura had a farm with the meanest chickens in the world.

Today was cookout day at Mom and Curtis's house. Everyone came, except for Big Momma, Grandpa, and Uncle Clarence, who was the oldest of all the children. Uncle Clarence had a different father because of a rape that Big Momma had suffered. Uncle Clarence always seemed distant and in his own world; for some reason, Big Momma would never leave any of us kids alone with him. However, he was always nice and not like the monsters.

Auntie June attended with her usual entourage, which included her boyfriend of the week and two of his friends. Everyone was eating, playing cards and dominoes, and the music was so loud you could hear it for blocks while everyone sang along to Kool and the Gang. Suddenly, we heard Curtis cursing at one of the guys with Auntie June for flirting with my mom. The next thing we knew, the man was being beaten with a large car jack; blood was splattering everywhere, and

PAPER CHASE

everyone was screaming. The guy began to shake as if he was being electrocuted, then just stopped moving. It was so quiet you could hear a pin drop. All the adults quickly held a conference. I saw them roll the guy up in a carpet, clean up the blood, and they never spoke of it again. I kept wondering what happened to that man. Was he alive? Did he end up with brain damage?

As if there weren't enough traumatic events happening, I was terrified because Big Momma was getting even sicker from diabetes. Auntie June was coming over more often, but she was being mean to Big Momma, yelling for money and demanding valuables, including the use of a fancy 1972 Cadillac Coupe Deville that Big Momma owned.

PAPER CHASE

CHAPTER FOUR

One evening, I was playing Connect Four with my sister Stephanie. I had received this game for my twelfth birthday. Suddenly, a loud knock startled us at the back window of our apartment. When we looked out, no one was there. Ten minutes later, two policemen were knocking at our door. I heard one of them ask, "Were you guys just knocking at the window?" They looked at Curtis in confusion and replied, "Why would we knock at the window?"

Then, I heard my mother scream, a sound filled with a terror I had never heard from her before. The mean man was even crying. What on earth was happening?

The police delivered the devastating news that Big Momma had passed away. They had to come and tell us in person because Curtis was too cheap to afford a phone. Upon hearing the news, the pain sank deep into my stomach, and I eventually

PAPER CHASE

threw up. I lost control of my emotions and tears. It became a troubling pattern for me; whenever something upset me, I would black out. The next thing I remembered was sitting on Big Momma's bed in her house. I could still smell her; the entire room carried the scent of Caress soap and Chloe perfume. I felt as if she was the only person in the world who truly loved me, and now she was gone.

Although Big Momma had been ill from diabetes, the circumstances surrounding her death were very suspicious and pointed to Auntie June. Big Momma had everything arranged for her final arrangements, as if she had known she was going to die. She left instructions for the funeral home, her clothing, wig, and even the colors to be used. However, she left out two crucial things: what to do with her home and her vehicles.

During the funeral preparations, it became apparent that most of Big Momma's children were addicted to crack, except for my aunts—Latrice, who lived in California; Dee, who was disabled and lived with Latrice; Rhonda, who lived in San

PAPER CHASE

Francisco with her husband; and my mom, Sharon. My uncles, Clarence, Isaiah, and Jeff, tried to appear somewhat helpful, but Auntie June had changed dramatically due to her addiction. I feared that this was just the beginning of trouble, and things would become much worse now that Big Momma was gone.

On the way to Timbuktu, I rode in the family car with my Grandpa, Aunt Laura, and Reverend Cooks. Aunt Laura kept me close to her the whole time. She talked about how much my Big Momma loved and cared for me, and she asked if my mom or anyone else had gone through the paperwork in the file cabinet yet. I was only twelve, so I had no idea what paperwork they had looked at. It rained heavily on the way home from the cemetery.

Soon, Curtis, my mother, my little sister, and I moved back to Phoenix into my Big Momma's home. My Aunt Latrice relocated from California with her son and my favorite uncle, Isaiah, and rented out the house that Curtis had purchased before our unexpected trip to Denver. The conflict began when

PAPER CHASE

Auntie June had not paid the mortgage on Big Momma's home for over six months. She had sold most of her valuables, and the very expensive luxury car that belonged to Big Momma was missing. My mom and Curtis started working to catch up on the mortgage, which was even more difficult because all the important documents had been scattered throughout the house. You wouldn't believe it, but the other relatives were so concerned about who would inherit the house that they refused to help save it.

After many arguments, fights, and calls to the police, Uncle Jeff and Aunt June eventually moved out of Big Momma's home. Auntie June relocated to some projects that my mom used to say she was afraid to drive through, even during the day. Auntie June had three children, with a fourth on the way. Something happened between my mom and Auntie June because they barely spoke to each other. Every time Auntie June's name came up, my mom cried and became upset. I overheard Isaiah say that everyone knew June had done something to Big

PAPER CHASE

Momma. Auntie June gave birth to her fourth child, a girl, who, for some reason, looked exactly like Curtis, my mom's husband. I wondered why this child resembled him so much. Other family members joked that June had "marked" the baby, implying that since June fought with Curtis so often and disliked him, her punishment was to have a child that looked like him. It was like something out of a Jerry Springer show. I didn't think Big Momma would have been pleased.

Several years passed, and eventually, Curtis and Mom realized they couldn't catch up on the back mortgage on the house. Curtis decided it would be smarter to buy a home in the same neighborhood, just around the corner. They ended up purchasing one of the largest and nicest houses right on the corner, close to Big Momma's house. Auntie Latrice and Curtis weren't getting along because she hadn't paid rent in months. So when we moved out of Big Momma's house, Latrice and her crew moved in to save it. Latrice was a lot like Big Momma—a hard worker who liked nice things—

but her house was filthy. When it came to cooking, she couldn't boil water without burning it. In fact, the only thing she could cook was spaghetti, and that wasn't all that great, either.

Latrice usually had a lot going on at her place, with plenty of company and unusual visitors from California. Dee lived with Latrice because she was developmentally disabled. Apparently, she had contracted polio as a young child, which caused her developmental issues; she was also deaf and mute. Isaiah was addicted to crack but still managed to do mechanic work and spend time with me and my sister. Even though he had a drug problem, he didn't act strange around us. The only way we knew he had issues was because he was frequently in and out of jail for theft-related crimes. Uncle Jeff lived there as well but was often at the county hospital due to stomach issues, probably because he drank Southern Comfort like it was water.

PAPER CHASE

Latrice must have come into some money because she eventually saved Big Momma's house. She started living a lavish lifestyle—buying cars, furniture, and shopping all the time—doing pretty much whatever she wanted.

Shortly after my thirteenth birthday, we received a call to come to the county hospital. It was Uncle Jeff. He had cirrhosis of the liver, and the doctors said an operation was his only chance to save his life. We waited for hours in the waiting area. After about 12 hours, the surgeons emerged, still in their operating outfits. They both had blank looks on their faces, and the first words they spoke were, "I'm sorry." Screams erupted throughout the hospital. Jeff did not survive the surgery. Another funeral was planned, and we took another long trip to the cemetery in Timbuktu. Uncle Isaiah was in prison at the time and had to be brought to the service by guards; he was shackled as if he were a criminal. This was the first funeral I had attended where it didn't rain. I wondered if there was some connection between death and rain.

PAPER CHASE

After the service, Aunt Rhonda moved back from San Francisco, and Uncle Clarence relocated from Los Angeles. With everyone back in the same city, things should have improved, right? Wrong!

It was my eighth-grade graduation, and it feels like a blur. I barely scraped by with passing grades to graduate because I was consumed with adult problems. I was worried about our living situation because of my mom's unstable husband, and I was concerned about my aunt's children, especially after Ricky died. I took the city bus to my graduation alone. After the ceremony, as I boarded the bus, I saw all my classmates taking pictures with their families and getting into cars to celebrate.

Once I turned fourteen, I could participate in a summer work program. My first job was as a receptionist for the City of Phoenix Fire Department. I couldn't believe my eyes when I received my first paycheck—I had earned $300! I was eager to spend it at the mall with Aunt Latrice, who seemed to favor boys for some reason and was generally rude to the other girls in our family. She loved me, but she didn't seem to care much for most girls. I was close to her son, who taught me how to fight and tested my skills daily. After spending my $300, I found myself waiting in the food court while they continued shopping.

Later, back at the house, I asked Latrice how she could afford to spend money so carelessly. What she showed me next changed the course of my life: the paper chase was on. She introduced me to a small white rock-like substance known as crack, which had half the neighborhood acting like zombies. My cousin was knowledgeable about the game; he had learned from his mom. He explained everything to me, from how to cook it to how to sell it and get more.

There was a rumor that my biological dad always played dominoes with Rochelle's dad, who lived down the street. Rochelle and I got along, but she was a good girl, and we didn't hang out much. She liked everything I didn't: school, church, and her mom. When I asked her about the rumor, she

PAPER CHASE

confirmed it was true that my biological dad was friends with her dad. Apparently, I was a mistake, and he wanted nothing to do with me because his wife wouldn't approve. Rumor has it that he had kids all over the valley. Well, if he didn't want me, I didn't want him, I thought. I made sure to keep track of when he would visit Rochelle, so there was no chance of us ever running into each other. I never wanted to lay eyes on this man; I knew he didn't claim me or want anything to do with me.

I stayed employed, but it was just a front for my side business. By the age of sixteen, I had become very popular and formed a rap group called P.P.I.A. (Party People in Action). The group included Ladona, who lived on my street and had been my best friend since the sixth grade, and Yvette, whose dad was a policeman, so we had to be cautious with her. We were known by our nicknames: I was Snoopy, Ladona was Baby Doll, and Yvette was Smiley. We performed all over the city and consistently won talent shows. I covered our travel expenses and our outfits, which typically consisted

PAPER CHASE

of sweatshirts, Levi's, and Timberland boots that matched our sweatshirts.

Somehow, Ladona discovered where all the money was coming from and the secret behind the white substance. Once she knew, it became all about the almighty dollar for her. I even bought my first car with cash, an '85 Sedan DeVille, but I had to park it down the street so my mom wouldn't find out what I was up to.

One day, I was driving through the Southside with my little sister, Stephanie. As we approached a red light, we spotted a car that looked like my mother's Cadillac. To my dismay, it was indeed my mother! You should have seen the look on her face when she realized it was us. She yelled, "Pull over!" and motioned with her hand angrily.

What would my grandmother have thought of me? The same drug I was glorifying was the same epidemic wreaking havoc on millions of families. This life was becoming dangerous. I had to transform into someone I was not: mean, cruel, and money-hungry. I needed some muscle because I was not cut out for this rough lifestyle.

During a re-up, I was introduced to Baby He, an OG from San Diego, California, who was part of the Skyline crew "Bloods." The Skyline Pirus (SLP), also known as the East Side Pirus (Rollin 80s), is primarily an African-American blood gang located throughout Southeast San Diego. Law enforcement considers them to be the largest blood gang in San Diego. The Skyline (Meadow 68th and 69th Street) has been on the police radar since the 1970s. The Skyline Pirus allows members from different ethnic groups to join, including Polynesian/Pacific Islanders, Asians, and Mexican-Americans.

Because of my connection with him, just hearing his name on the block ignited fear. Things were moving too fast, and I knew I should slow down; I had enemies and was associating with all the wrong people. However, my affiliation with the Bloods kept me safe and earned me respect.

PAPER CHASE

I became the girlfriend of a guy from San Diego named Tony. He was ruthless, with the nickname Diablo (the devil). Tony and I mostly went to parties and occasionally to the movies, but he barely let me out of his sight. When I found out I was pregnant, Tony started to dictate my every move. At first, I didn't mind, as my conscience needed a break from the drug game. It was much easier selling fish dinners. Instead of me having to deal drugs, Tony took care of that while I figured out how to make money selling various documents and the occasional fish plate.

I moved out of my mom's and Curtis's house and into Tony's place, where he was nineteen. Once I moved in with him, things got real—quickly. He would sometimes bring home a good amount of money, but when he was home, we would argue about how he treated me and his habit of running around with other women. I can't tell you how many females called and texted me. They would send me a "911" page, expecting me to call back, and some

PAPER CHASE

even approached me at the club, asking if I knew him.

That same year, Tony's mother was found dead in the desert. She had been murdered by her boyfriend, beaten to death. Tony knew my history with relationships and had promised from the start that he would never put his hands on me, and he kept that promise. We were expecting twins, and one child was the last thing I needed, let alone two at seventeen, especially since I was already helping take care of Auntie June's kids. Auntie June would leave all four of those kids alone at night, and even worse, she would leave them with random men. My mom and I would check on them and bring them food.

One day, I was feeling troubled and barely slept at all. My stomach was upset and in knots, and for some strange reason, I just wanted Tony to stay home with me. At the time, there was a violent turf battle going on between the Hilltop crew, some guys from the Vistas, Park South, and the Broadway Gangsters. We weren't hurting for money, so I told him I wasn't feeling well, hoping he would choose to stay home. He said he already had plans. "I bet you do," I thought, feeling frustrated, and I yelled at him.

Tony and I argued back and forth about his unfaithful ways; I called him names I'd never called anyone before, and he stormed out. I was furious with Tony and so tired of being his little girl toy who cooked and cleaned. I wanted a real relationship.

At 3 a.m., my phone rang—it was Tony's cousin. "Hello," I answered, still half-asleep. His cousin said, "I've got some bad news, Snoop. Those crab-ass fools killed my relative!" I sat up in bed in disbelief; I couldn't believe that anyone would catch him slipping. With all the driving he used to have me doing between Arizona and San Diego, I knew he was usually the first one to shoot. I was upset that he had been shot and killed, but I wasn't devastated. I felt safe and financially stable; it seemed like Tony had practically forced me to be his girlfriend anyway. One day, he just declared, "You're my woman now, come on," and I followed.

PAPER CHASE

The week after the funeral, I suffered a miscarriage of both babies. One had slipped into the fallopian tube, damaging it so severely that my prognosis for ever having children again was grim. After being released from the hospital, I returned to my mom's home to recover. Big Momma wouldn't approve of my behavior; I knew this would break her heart. To change my lifestyle, I got a job at a local grocery store as a carry-out.

It was there that I met Lavelle. I had seen him around; he grew up near the house where Latrice rented from Curtis. He was quiet and, while most guys considered him a square, the girls thought he was cute. He wasn't particularly interesting—he played video games and read comic books—but he was the first guy I found attractive aside from Roderick. Roderick lived down the street from my mom and taught me how to shoot dice, fire a pistol, and fight dirty. Both Roderick and Lavelle had long Jheri curls and seemed to have no shortage of girls interested in them.

PAPER CHASE

I continued working as a carry-out and kept to myself. I also regularly sent pictures and wrote several letters a week to Uncle Isaiah, who was still in prison. I later found out from some co-workers that Lavelle, along with many other guys, secretly had a crush on me. I was unaware of this at the time, but apparently, all the guys thought I was a prize. Unfortunately, I didn't think the same of myself.

Eventually, Lavelle mustered the courage to ask me out to lunch. I thought, "Lunch? Okay, he is a square!" We went out and started to date. Lavelle was nicer than most boys who were as handsome as he was and didn't seem overly concerned about sex, which relieved me because I wasn't an affectionate person, and sex wasn't enjoyable for me. In my opinion, sex was more for the guy and felt like a duty for me because I was a female.

I grew tired of working in the hot sun since the temperature was 240 degrees! So, I got an inside job as a waitress at a grocery store not far from the neighborhood. Ladona already worked

PAPER CHASE

there as a hostess, and I brought my sister Stephanie along with me. I was surprised they made any money at all. Between us giving away food and hitting the register, we probably got away with thousands of dollars each month. This was not good and was sure to come back to haunt me if I didn't stop. I always believed in karma. I'm sure those talks with Big Momma influenced my thinking. She would often say, "What's done in the dark will come to light." Ladona quit shortly after, as she was deep into the drug game by then. I only dealt every now and then to get extra money, but I wanted nothing to do with a life of drug dealing. Even my younger sister had started following in my footsteps by dealing drugs, which definitely wouldn't make Big Momma proud.

Early one morning, the hospital called and asked for my mom, who had already gone to work. The woman on the phone, who I guessed was white because her name was Cindy and she sounded like a valley girl, said, "Oh my God, you guys have a new baby!" She explained that Auntie June had given

PAPER CHASE

birth to a baby who was addicted to crack cocaine, and that Child Protective Services would take the child if no one over 18 in the family could come to get her. I quickly doctored up my birth certificate to make it say I was 18, even though I was only 17, and headed to the hospital. Just as I was leaving to go, my mom came home early from work, not feeling well. I explained the phone call, and we both rushed out together to get the baby. When we arrived, there was very little verification of our identities; in fact, I'm not sure if they even confirmed we were relatives. Apparently, Auntie June had told them to call my mom and had checked out before we could get there to avoid being sent to jail. The baby, named Candy, looked perfect, but her screams were like nothing I'd ever heard before—like she was in constant pain! She also resembled Curtis, my mom's husband. Deep down, I knew why... we all knew why.

My mother accepted responsibility for this infant. Both she and I took turns staying up with Candy, who cried for hours and experienced terrible

PAPER CHASE

withdrawal symptoms from crack. It was sure to be a long and difficult road filled with doctor appointments, medication, and psychiatric care for this child who hadn't asked to be brought into the world. A few days later, my mother and I decided to check on the other children belonging to Auntie June. When we arrived, the situation was unbelievable. There was filth everywhere—dirty clothes, no food. The children had been locked in the house for over a week and had found an opening through a small bathroom window. Apparently, the older two had been escaping through the window to steal food from a nearby grocery store. We took the children with us that day and were forced to involve Child Protective Services. The oldest child was placed in a group home, the second oldest—a boy—was placed with Aunt Latrice, and Candy stayed with my mom. Two of the children were placed in my custody, so I moved out and returned to my own apartment in the building where Tony and I had lived.

PAPER CHASE

CHAPTER FIVE

Lavelle and I were becoming serious.

Shortly after my eighteenth birthday, he presented me with a beautiful promise ring, and soon a miracle happened—we conceived a child. Shortly after that, he asked me to marry him. Lavelle was still working at the local grocery store where we had met. Even though he had received a promotion, he feared that he wouldn't have the resources to provide for me, my cousins, and the new baby on the way. To take care of me and our miracle daughter, who was born after my miscarriage when I was told I might not be able to conceive, Lavelle enlisted in the armed forces that year.

Once Lavelle returned from overseas, he was stationed in Coronado Bay, California, a suburb of San Diego. During this time, he visited us in Phoenix until he could move us to San Diego with him. There is a God! My mom finally left Curtis after eighteen years of beatdowns, humiliation, and infidelity. As I was preparing to move with Lavelle, she took care

PAPER CHASE

of the two girls in my custody, and of course, the baby, Candy, still lived with her. My life was about to take a new direction that I had never even imagined, enhanced by the possibility of moving overseas with Lavelle. I was overjoyed to be joining my soon-to-be husband, so I headed for the coast.

Everything was set up and ready to go in San Diego: our apartment, a car, and even food in the fridge. I admired this man more than he knew. He didn't have good parenting examples, but he was turning out to be one of the best fathers I had ever witnessed in my life thus far. My examples had been James from "Good Times," Cliff Huxtable from "The Cosby Show," and Fred Sanford from "Sanford and Son." We conceived our second child, and I went into labor early while watching "Hellraiser" — I guess it literally scared the hell out of me.

Once our second miracle daughter was born, he would tell me to take a break while he stayed up with the baby at night. I didn't even work and mostly slept during the day with the baby, yet he still wanted to let me rest, even after he'd worked all day. Soon, I was ready for shopping and eager to hit some of those swap meets I had heard so much about.

Ladonna, my best friend, was around. Yaaas!!! She was in San Diego, and we were out celebrating her birthday. We went to a swap meet, and my eyes nearly popped out of my head. My mind screamed to run, but my legs wouldn't move. It was Baby He, the OG from Skyline, all smiles and inviting us to a BBQ at Skyline Park later that day. A guilty feeling washed over me, but the excitement of being with friends outweighed the boredom of sitting at home.

Once we arrived at the BBQ, we were greeted by several guys who treated us like celebrities, even having some women fix our plates. I thought, "Ain't this some shit?" The women preparing our food weren't happy about it either. I told Ladonna I wasn't eating anything they fixed—who knows what they did to our food when we weren't looking? But her crazy self said, "Fuck that, I'm hungry."

PAPER CHASE

Baby He had a mischievous glint in his eye, fueled by his love for the hustle. I could sense he had plans for me. That day, I met Ronald Black, a tall, muscular young man from Skyline who had earned respect from even the OGs for his work. The cycle resumed. Baby He had all kinds of scams in the works that needed my skills with illegal documents. As soon as Lavelle would get home, I would be off to the races. Baby He had everything from counterfeiting to fake checks, credit cards, and robbing ballers from other gangs. Ronald Black and I became partners in crime, "Bonnie and Clyde," sometimes making thousands of dollars in one day, which was more than enough for me.

Again, I thought about what Big Momma would say about my lifestyle. She always talked about my potential and how smart I was. I realized I was using my intelligence for the wrong things; I could not continue down this path. I was sure she was turning over in her grave over my choices. Lavelle and I had grown apart because of my relationship with Ronald Black and the crimes I was committing, which I had never spoken about.

I thought it would be best to return home to Arizona because I was beginning to feel like someone was following me, and I constantly had to watch my own back. Lavelle and I separated, but not before Ronald Black and I pulled off one more "lick." For those unfamiliar with the term, a "lick" is a robbery that results in a significant pay-off. We had our eyes on a wealthy gentleman, with whom I had enjoyed dinner several times. I didn't want to go through with our plan, but we were already in too deep.

On the specified night, at the appointed time, this gentleman picked me up for our date. Little did he know, his worst fears were about to manifest. He was beaten, tied up, and taken back to his beachfront property to open his safe. Everything went as planned, except for the fact that we didn't truly know who this wealthy man was. Was this a setup? Sometimes, those you watch are already watching you. After the news broke that we had robbed the wrong powerful individual, we hid for two days. Then, under the cover of darkness, we loaded up a moving truck and left San Diego, guarded by several OGs with machine guns while I carried a Mac 11. It was a horrifying experience; I feared for my life and the lives of my two children. I prayed to God for our safety and vowed never to engage in such activities again. Later, we heard through the grapevine that the wealthy gentleman never figured out who we were.

I was back in hot Arizona with Ronald Black and my children, so it was time to get back to business. As I would say, "let me brush my shoulders off." I needed to find a job and make some money; I had to set things right for my girls. I had always been someone who could come up with solutions during tough situations. The girls liked Ronald; he was funny and had a kind heart. I cared for Ronald as a friend, but I was aware of many secrets between us. I knew who he was—a criminal—after all, I was the driver! I knew how he treated women and that one woman was never

PAPER CHASE

enough for him, which made it hard for me to trust him. I don't know why I settled for him and crossed the line between friends and something more. Was it for financial stability, or did I want to keep our secrets hidden?

Two years later, Ronald and I conceived a son. A miracle? Yes? But I felt ashamed because I knew this would diminish any hope of reconciling with Lavelle. I asked Lavelle to forgive me for my poor judgment and infidelity with Ronald Black, and we parted ways, never to look back. He was a good, decent man who deserved better than what I had given him. I was sure karma would find me on a lonely road for the way I treated my blessing. Lavelle continued to support his children financially, going above and beyond what the courts required.

By the time my son was born, Ronald and I had separated because I was tired of all the women calling my house. He was furious that I didn't give my son his first name; however, I gave him Ronald's middle and last name, of course. Ronald moved down south to live with one of his uncles and would

PAPER CHASE

never return to Arizona. He came back once a month for a while to see his "Baby Boy," as he called him, but he never sent me a dime.

Around the same time, I met Tiffany VanSnowden, a down-to-earth woman from the Bay Area who was focused on making money, legally. That year, I began working at a local phone company that paid its employees well. Seriously, I thought some of them were involved in illegal activities. I reached a point in my life where I couldn't afford to keep knowing the wrong people, especially men. I was pretty attractive, and very few women could outdress me. Although I wasn't interested in telemarketing, I knew I had to do what I had to do. That's when I met Keith.

Keith wasn't particularly attractive, but he had a great smile and a magnetic personality. He could put on a show! I think because he was so likable, most people overlooked his appearance. He was 6'1" and weighed at least 400 pounds, with a large, round face, sunken eyes, and dark circles

PAPER CHASE

under his eyes. Despite this, he was a successful supervisor at the company.

Keith began to pursue me; it took me three months to even consider going out with him. He had two children and said he was okay with the fact that I had three children, one of whom was a small baby at home. He wined and dined me, and when we went out to clubs, you would have thought he was "Big Poppa," only slightly better looking—though not by much.

We dated for several months, and he was a perfect gentleman, always opening doors and giving me as many gifts as he could afford. He wasn't my type physically, but I was tired of being tossed around by those handsome, self-absorbed guys. I won't lie—sometimes I still had to make a booty call because Keith wasn't my type and I hadn't agreed to commit to him at that point.

I wanted a stable relationship, someone I could grow old with, so I began to look past physical appearance and allow myself to consider

PAPER CHASE

falling in love with this man's heart. Keith was huge, and his body type resembled a Tasmanian devil. His face was round and chubby, with dark circles under his eyes, sort of like a raccoon.

PAPER CHASE

CHAPTER SIX

I was 25 when Isaiah was released from prison, and I was overjoyed because of my memories of working on cars with him and his traveling to Denver to see us. He stepped out of the joint with cash, bought a Cadillac, and kept moving forward. I only hoped he wouldn't quench his thirst for crack, especially since he was going to be living with Latrice, who was still selling drugs.

So much has happened within our family since Big Momma's passing. My cousin, Latrice's son, had received a 20-year sentence for armed robbery, along with Auntie June's only son, who was just a kid at the time. Auntie June's son had been living with Aunt Latrice and was swept up in the situation when my cousin decided to commit the crime. He had chronic asthma, so when the robbery went down, he had an attack, and my cousin left him behind. The way our justice system worked, the phrase "I was along for the ride" was not a good defense; he received significant time in prison.

PAPER CHASE

Our family didn't feel like a real family anymore; no one liked each other, and there was constant fighting and backbiting. It was a mess! A family barbecue could be just the thing to bring us back together and celebrate Isaiah's homecoming. Isaiah, whose birthday was on Valentine's Day, was very likable and had many talents. He could fix everything from cars to home air conditioners. However, he seemed strange this time. He wasn't comfortable around large groups of people, family or not. He seemed to want to be alone. I loved him and missed him so much that I became his constant companion. We went to the casino, out to eat, to look at cars he planned to fix, and went shopping whenever I could convince him to buy something for himself.

One rainy day, we had planned to go to the auction because he wanted to buy a few cars and sell them. I headed over to pick him up; I was usually the driver since I knew all the backstreets. I entered the house and yelled, "What's up, unc!" like I normally did, but he seemed especially down. I asked, "What's wrong, unc?" He said, "Sit down, niecey," which is what my aunts and uncles called me. I braced myself for the news; I could tell it wasn't good. Just then, Latrice walked in, and he quickly changed the subject, pretending to ask about a lady he wanted me to hook him up with. I played along, but I couldn't shake the feeling that he had something important to tell me.

One morning, while I was getting ready for work, the phone rang. It was Stephanie, my little sister. She instructed me to turn on the news. What I saw ripped through me like the cold Chicago wind, known as "The Hawk." I felt the life leave my body momentarily. Isaiah lay lifeless under a black body bag on the freeway. The report said he was high on cocaine and had been sprayed with pepper spray; he died as a result of his reaction to the pepper spray.

It rained heavily the day of the funeral. I drove his Cadillac alone to the cemetery, listening to Mary J. Blige's "My Life" the whole way. Uncle Isaiah didn't look anything like himself, lying cold and still in that casket. I could tell he was troubled when he died; he literally had frown lines on his forehead. I couldn't help but wonder what he wanted to tell me that day at the house. Would I ever know? One thing was certain: I felt his unspoken words were somehow connected to the way he died, and I was determined to find out.

I overheard Latrice on the phone with a lawyer, and I suspected she had sued the city for wrongful death, but no one in the family ever saw a dime of the money she received.

Keith had claimed, "I was the one." He wanted to settle down and build a life together. I suspected that he was feeling lonely since his two children had moved to Indiana with their mother. I could see my dream of a family life becoming a little closer to reality. However, my lack of physical attraction to Keith influenced my emotional feelings about him. I enjoyed our time together, but he sometimes made me uncomfortable because he was always all over me.

PAPER CHASE

Keith became my rock; he was supportive of everything I did. He worked hard and enjoyed going out, which made him a lot of fun to be around. However, I began to feel the weight of life's choices catching up to me, or what some would call karma. I started experiencing money issues and struggled to pay my bills and provide for my children. Even with Lavelle's continued financial support, money was tight. Up to that point, I had been trying to save the world by helping anyone who asked for my assistance. I realized that going out to clubs, drinking Cognac, and frequently wearing those GUESS jeans certainly didn't help my budget. I had not learned how to budget or save money. It felt like I could get my idea of success out of my system, but the reality was that I was broke. Despite having helped a lot of people, no one came to my rescue. I couldn't even get my money back from people I had lent to in the past; nobody was answering the phone then! I remember being angry at one of my relatives because I couldn't even get back the $20 I lent him after three years. Ridiculous!

PAPER CHASE

I was embarrassed when I discovered I was pregnant with my fourth child, but I wasn't sure if Keith was the father due to a few factors. I was completely transparent with Keith about my concerns and told him exactly what was going on: 1. I was on the pill, 2. I thought we used a condom the one time we were together after I had made him wait seven months, and 3. I had been with one other guy during the time Keith and I were dating. I was supposed to be getting my life together and finding ways to become a better person, yet here I was, in a difficult situation. I didn't even know who the father of my baby was.

PAPER CHASE

CHAPTER SEVEN

I was stuck on the fact that if I hadn't made the wrong choices and cheated on Lavelle, this wouldn't be happening. Let me explain: guilt was consuming me—not because I wanted to be with Lavelle, but because he was one of the best human beings ever, and I had hurt him deeply with my actions. I reflected on everything, and I could see that everything I had gained while I was away from him was now gone: all the money, the car, the jewelry, the electronics, and the lowest blow—my clothes. We had been evicted from our apartment, and my only option was to rent one of Latrice's properties, a townhouse in the barrio. Don't get me wrong, it wasn't free just because she was my aunt; she wanted her rent, believe me! It was easier to rent from Latrice because of my bad credit.

Would you believe someone actually tried to break into the townhouse knowing I was there? Between the roaches and the thieves attempting to break in, I sat up all night with my .38 pistol in hand,

PAPER CHASE

waiting for those idiots to test me again. I felt disrespected and angry. The next morning, I went to find a storage facility to put my furniture in because I couldn't live like this. When I returned for my things, someone had already broken into the townhouse and taken the few valuables I had left. Determined not to break down, I brushed myself off, grabbed the rest of my belongings, and got going.

That night, my two daughters, my son, and I stayed at Keith's house. It just so happened his brother had been released from prison that same week. Keith had only told me negative things about his brother, mostly that he was a pervert and watched a lot of porn. I had always vowed that no monster would ever touch my girls. It had been a very traumatic week, and I was exhausted, both mentally and physically. Amid all the chaos, I found a higher-paying job and would be starting that following Monday at another phone company. Keith welcomed me and the children with open arms and a smile.

PAPER CHASE

I had already explained to him what had happened at the townhouse. He rolled out the sofa bed, and the children and I rested. Soon, his brother came in, and Keith wanted me to go into the bedroom with him, leaving my children vulnerable to someone I did not trust. I didn't want to tell Keith about my concerns regarding his brother, so he didn't understand why I wouldn't leave my kids on the couch alone. I was worried that the monster might come for them too.

The next morning was Sunday. Keith was still upset that I hadn't slept next to him, which led to an argument between us. I decided to gather my belongings and the kids and head to my mom's house, where she had recently remarried. Once outside, I felt deeply hurt and confused by the way Keith had spoken to me about sleeping on the couch. In a moment of frustration, I hit his bedroom window, which was in front of my car.

Suddenly, Keith jumped through the window and began to punch me in the head and face. He tore my shirt completely off and threw me to the

PAPER CHASE

ground, causing my legs to scrape against the rough surface while my children screamed from the car. In that moment of desperation, I grabbed my .38 revolver, and everything in me wanted to pull the trigger. But then, I blacked out.

When I arrived at my mom's house, I was beaten and bleeding. I hadn't heard her cry like that since Big Momma passed away. Without asking any questions, she immediately ran a bath with Epsom salt and aloe for me. Afterward, she bathed the kids, fed them, and put them to bed. Later, I told my mom about a stranger across the street who had been shouting, "Noooo, Stacey, don't do it!" I was sure the woman had called my name, but I had no idea who she was. After hearing that voice, I took my finger off the trigger and drove away, barely recalling the long thirty-minute journey to my mom's house.

I started my new job the next morning with a plan to stabilize my family, man or not. I was thinking no man; they only inflict pain on me. I met a really cool girl named Agelique Peters. She had five

PAPER CHASE

kids and was doing her best to provide for them, but her house was a mess; I mean, there was stuff everywhere. Nonetheless, Agelique was good people. I needed my friends more than ever. I was still close to Ladonna, but Yvette had fallen off the face of the earth; no one had heard from her in years. Between my old friends and my two new friends, Tiffany and Agelique, they helped me through a very tough transition in my life.

I worked hard and had to get a house in my mother's name because an eviction was showing up on my credit report. I made arrangements to pay the judgment so that I could eventually restore my good name one day. The house was a remodeled ranch-style home in an area that was once upscale, with a large population of retired people. There was a HUGE lady named Heidi who lived next door to me—I'm talking some "Fee Fi Foe Fum" HUGE! Heidi was German and had to be 6'1" and weighed 275 pounds without an ounce of fat or flab. Heidi did a lot of yard work; sometimes, she would even clean my yard.

PAPER CHASE

I had met a nice couple at work, Clarence and Dee from Chicago. They offered to help me move my things out of storage and get settled in. Around this same time, I got back Auntie June's girls, whom I originally had custody of. While we were moving, Clarence disappeared with the moving truck for over a week. As a matter of fact, let me explain this: I forgot to mention that Clarence is a crackhead! The whole U-Haul went missing... When we finally located it, he had sold most of my things—clothes and all. Dee apologized for Clarence's addiction repeatedly and even tried to buy me things to make up for it, but I didn't hold her responsible. However, I was furious that she hadn't told me about her man's crackhead tendencies. In a way, I couldn't help but think that this was payback for my own past of selling drugs. This was the second wardrobe I had to replace within a year—what the hell?

I spoke with Keith every now and then, because after a thorough investigation and backtracking, he was indeed the father of the child I was carrying. The next time I saw Keith was at the hospital after I had given birth to our daughter. He was amazed at how much she resembled his mother and his five year old daughter -.

After having the baby, I needed some air. About a month later, my friends and I went to Zorro's, a local club that was popular at the time. I was dancing and minding my own business when suddenly, I was snatched off the dance floor by my hair by none other than Keith. I was swinging and trying to fight back, but he had a grip on my throat. Finally, he literally lifted me off the ground and backed off. I told him to only approach me if it was about his daughter.

I started reflecting on the opportunity to have a family and somehow blamed myself for what happened. I thought I shouldn't have been out at the club so soon after having the baby. Two weeks later, I tried to reach him, but he was hard to find. Being true to the game, I decided to confront him and went to his house. When I arrived, I noticed there was no one parked in my designated spot and

PAPER CHASE

thought it was my turn to act up. To this day, I'm unsure why I did what I did. I knocked on the door, and his weak roommate answered and said Keith wasn't there. In that moment, I blacked out!

Before I knew it, I had burst through the door and found him in bed with some woman he wouldn't let me see. At that time, I was convinced it was because she was unattractive. I knew I was the most attractive woman he had ever dated. The next morning, feeling brokenhearted, I went to church seeking answers. My life was beginning to feel unbearably painful. Was this normal? I was incredibly hurt because Keith and I had discussed trying to rebuild our relationship and start a family together. Keith also attended church that day, and after a long talk, we decided to give it another shot. I felt it was worth it since we shared a child and he expressed deep remorse for hurting me, assuring me he wouldn't hit me again. I'll never forget crying at the altar that Sunday morning.

PAPER CHASE

However, his jealousy and controlling nature did not cease; in fact, they worsened. Keith became more overbearing than ever. This was turning into a new nightmare. Each time he hit me, he would try to have sex to make up for it, which made me feel like I was dealing with one of those monsters I had known as a child. My fear began to resurface. One year on my birthday, he decided to invite his friends over to celebrate with us. I didn't have any friends to invite because that always seemed to trigger a fight with Keith. During the party, while reflecting on my life, I became very depressed. I felt tears welling up in my eyes, so I excused myself to the bedroom to regain my composure.

While sitting at a small student desk in our bedroom, Keith entered and noticed I was crying. Without saying a word, he balled up his fist and hit me hard on the side of my head, making me feel as though my eardrum had burst. All I could hear was a loud ringing noise. As I lay on the floor in a pool of blood, he left the room as if nothing had happened.

PAPER CHASE

The force of Keith's blow left a large gash above my right eyebrow. Just as I was getting up off the floor, Keith's friend's wife came in to check on me. She let out a low scream when she saw the blood on my face. She helped me to the restroom to try to stop the bleeding and suggested we call an ambulance. I was still struggling to hear and told her I would drive myself to the emergency room and asked her to tell the other guests that I wasn't feeling well so they wouldn't see my face.

I drove myself to the hospital that night and told the emergency room staff that I had fallen. They questioned me thoroughly, and it was clear they didn't believe me. I ended up receiving 22 stitches in my eye and had a ruptured eardrum. After that incident, I became extremely cautious around Keith, carefully watching what I said, how I said it, and to whom I spoke. It was like walking on eggshells every day. The children had to do the same because, instead of hitting them when they did something wrong, he would take it out on me for trying to protect them. How could I allow myself to become the type of person I had hated as a child? I had become my mother.

Soon, my family alienated me because they didn't understand why I stayed with someone I was afraid of. They were tired of watching me remain with a man who was abusing me. I felt lost and did not love myself. I had experienced many difficult situations, but I had vowed never to become like my mother. As time passed, my only confidants became my new friends, Tiffany VanSnowden—a loyal friend from the Bay Area—and Agelique Peters.

My Auntie June's two daughters decided to move in with Latrice because of the constant fighting. My children were always unhappy, and so was I. They were the only reason I didn't take my own life. I remember sitting in the bathroom, contemplating taking prescription medicine. I glanced at a blade and considered that option, but I was too afraid to inflict that much pain on myself. However, wasn't I already inflicting pain on myself by staying with someone who had pretended to be someone else in the beginning? He promised to

PAPER CHASE

protect me and nurture me, but instead, he was destroying me.

Oh, the agony and anguish I felt were almost unbearable. I felt unwanted, unloved, and unappreciated. I constantly asked my children about sexual abuse to ensure no one was touching them inappropriately, especially Keith. His behavior was so unpredictable that I didn't know if I could even trust him, particularly since he reminded me of terrifying figures from my past.

"God, please forgive me for the wrong I have done to others and for any hearts I may have broken," I cried out. "Is this karma for the way I treated Lavelle?" I wondered. Things continued to spiral on an up-and-down path for years; there would be good days, bad days, and really bad days.

PAPER CHASE

CHAPTER EIGHT

On February 14th, 1997, Isaiah's birthday, Keith proposed. A small voice inside me whispered, "Run, fool, run; too much time has already been spent." Despite that, I said "yes." I envisioned the perfect family: a husband, a wife, kids, a dog, a house, and two cars.

1. I believed that this was the way to earn God's blessing on our relationship.

2. I thought marriage was the key to emotional and financial stability.

My hobby was catering, so I was more than ready to plan my own fabulous wedding. My friends Tiffany and Agelique were by my side throughout the process. Tiffany was the fashion expert and knew all the hot clubs, while Agelique shared my passion for catering and party planning; she had connections everywhere. With Tiffany's approval, Agelique chose the colors, the seamstress, the beautician, the favors, and the centerpieces. She even arranged for her boyfriend, Edward, with whom she shared a son, to make our wedding cake. Meanwhile, Tiffany organized the bachelorette party and our girls' night out, both of which were overshadowed by Keith's jealousy.

The ups and downs during the wedding planning caused us to change the wedding date once, even after we had already sent out the invitations.

The day before the wedding was chaotic. My girls and I were running around picking up dresses, jewelry, and makeup. Agelique insisted that I buy MAC makeup. Normally, I only wore lip gloss, but I thought, "You only live once." As we headed to the mall to pick up our shoes, we hit a bump while coming through an intersection, and all of our dresses—the bridal gown, bridesmaid dresses, and flower girl dress—flew out of the trunk and down the street. Thankfully, the dresses were in plastic; Tiffany held back traffic while Agelique and I gathered them from the street.

PAPER CHASE

After we left the mall, we got onto the freeway for our next stop. Suddenly, we heard a loud "pop" that sounded like a gunshot, making us duck instinctively. The steering wheel began to shake violently. We had a flat tire. I panicked and called Latrice to use her AAA, which I frequently did. Once we resolved that, we were back on track and headed to the beautician, who turned out to be a talented gay black man working in his kitchen. I thought to myself, "Is this a sign? This is some bullshit," but he ended up doing an amazing job on our hair.

On the day of the wedding, everything was going smoothly and on time. The food was being provided by our church, and my friends had everything else under control. I only needed to get dressed. However, I received a message that our 1985 Limited Edition LeSabre, which we nicknamed Big Smokey, had caught fire while Keith and one of the groomsmen were in route to the wedding. Apparently, they managed to put out the fire with

PAPER CHASE

his friend's water hose, waited for the car to cool down, and then continued on their way.

Finally, it was time to start. Angelique had asked the coordinator for help, and she came to the dressing room to get me. I heard "The Art of Noise" playing, which meant my girls were swaying their way toward the altar. Then I heard "Ribbon in the Sky," which signaled that it was my turn to proceed. I took a deep breath and peeked out. I saw about 50 people in attendance when we had planned for 150. My heart dropped into my feet, and I felt light-headed and sick, as if someone were stabbing me in the stomach.

Reality hit me as I thought, none of these people are my family. One of Keith's brothers and some of his friends from work were there, but most of the guests were our church family. I began to cry, my heart felt ripped in half. They tried to force me to choose between them and Keith, and neither of my daughters wanted me to marry him; yet there they were, standing by my side. I blocked out all that negativity and pulled myself together. We had spent

PAPER CHASE

good, hard-earned money on this event, and I was determined to enjoy it.

The rest of the night felt like a fairytale—no kids, a toast at the house, and many promises made. We headed off to the after-reception party, which was being held at an upscale club uptown.

I stayed active in the church, participating in any activity I thought could help me become a better person. Despite that, we continued to have a very violent home life, and I kept praying, asking God to bless our relationship. I was sure God had forgiven me for the wrongs I had committed in the past, but I was still living in hell. My mother hadn't spoken to me for about seven months, but she called when Latrice told her I was pregnant with my fifth child.

Throughout the pregnancy, I developed a strong hatred for Keith and felt so ill that I could hardly eat or sleep. He was still abusive, and I was hospitalized once due to toxemia. I was miserable. One night, while I was cooking greasy hamburgers,

PAPER CHASE

my water broke. I heard a voice say, "It's on now." Full-speed ahead, Keith and I were on our way to the hospital, but first we had to pick up Latrice. She had witnessed the birth of all my children, and according to her, it was her "assignment."

I was in labor for 18 hours—the longest and most painful experience of my life. Finally, my 4-pound miracle was born. She had swallowed a little meconium but was healthy. I insisted on having a tubal ligation immediately.

More ups and downs, black eyes and bruises. I decided I had had enough. I had asked Keith to leave many times, yet I stayed. This time, after the recent beating I received after church on a Sunday while holding our youngest daughter, I was certain I had reached my limit. Keith had punched me full force in the jaw with a closed fist. For months, my face went from hurting to numb, and some days I could barely open my mouth.

PAPER CHASE

Money was not really an issue at that point; I qualified for my own place and left Keith. Agelique and her entire family came over while Keith was at work and helped me clear out our large home in just three hours—no joke! I moved into an upscale apartment in Tempe, marking the beginning of a new life for me. I had a good job at a credit card company, so I wasn't worried about paying the bills. My mom and little sister both recommended that I not speak to Keith for a while, and I agreed. I wasn't feeling well from that last beating, and my mom would bring me pain pills; it was the only way I could sleep. I started to wonder if the pain in my jaw could be from my wisdom tooth. I realized I needed to see a dentist, but I didn't have dental insurance. Why wouldn't I take advantage of the benefits I had? My mindset was simple-minded; I didn't want the cost of insurance cutting into my paycheck.

It was clear that Keith had control over many aspects of my life. He influenced my actions, my friends, my personality, my thinking, and my judgment. I had not only been a victim of physical abuse but also mental abuse. I avoided Keith for weeks until I finally gave in and took his call. What was wrong with me? Why was I listening to him? Why was I even considering what he suggested? Keith told me his mother was very ill and that he had an opportunity to transfer to Memphis to be closer to her. I agreed to give him another chance for all the wrong reasons: the kids, whom I started to call "The Coconut Crew," his family, and financial stability. The truth was, the situation was not good for the kids nor stable for anyone. I had fallen in love with his family because they had the close relationships that I knew families were supposed to have, but I had never personally experienced that type of family until I met them. That little voice in my head kept saying, "Run, fool, run."

I called my mom to let her know that we would be moving to Memphis. I also called Tiffany and Agelique. Everyone gave me the same advice: "You should not go." My mom was very angry but said she would support my decision this time. My

PAPER CHASE

girls always had my back, no matter what. Keith and I headed to Memphis to find a place and see the city. We flew into St. Louis to drive down to Illinois and visit his family for a few days before heading to Memphis. It was beautiful, but to be honest, I was in a daze. I couldn't believe I was about to move across the country with a man I didn't know if I could trust.

After looking at a few places in Memphis, we drove down to Mississippi, about two hours away, to see some of his mother's side of the family. Once we arrived, he introduced me to cousins he hadn't seen in years, but their dialect was so thick I could barely understand them. I just shook my head and tried to smile, despite the pain in my face. I asked Keith to take me back to the hotel so I could take a pain pill and lie down. For some reason, the pain was becoming intense; if I had a pistol, I surely would have shot myself just to escape it.

PAPER CHASE

I called Keith's cell and told him I needed to go to the emergency room. After several hours, a young doctor who looked like Doogie Howser came into my room and informed me that my jaw was fractured. Fractured? How could that be? I remembered the incident that started the pain in the first place. It was the beating that caused me to leave and move into my own apartment. Oh my God, I thought, how will I explain this to my mom? My jaw was wired shut, and I was given all the pain medication money could buy. I had to keep my jaw wired for six weeks and could only have liquids to eat. I lost so much weight that Aunt Latrice spread a rumor that I was on crack. That really pissed me off! I entertained her rumor and told my cousins that she was selling it to me just to make my mom mad at Latrice.

Two months later, the weekend before we left for Memphis, my mom threw a party at her house. For some reason, there was a strange, sad feeling, almost like déjà vu. My mom could cook incredibly well, and I was hungry and ready to eat since I finally had my wires off. She always jokingly told me, "I taught you everything you know," which wasn't true, but arguing with her was futile. She prepared fried chicken, potato salad, cabbage, pasta salad, salmon, and biscuits. My household included me, Keith, and "The Coconut Crew." My girls were there too, along with my mom's new husband and Candy.

Keith's friend Boomer, a country boy from Texas, and his wife, a tall, laid-back woman from California, were there to see us off. We talked about the South and the different restaurants I might visit, especially Beale Street. I promised to send lots of pictures. We all ate, drank, and enjoyed ourselves. After cleaning up, we hugged, kissed, and cried before saying our goodbyes.

Keith arranged for some of his friends to help us load the truck, and since I was the master packer, it wasn't a difficult job. Two of his brothers would drive the moving truck and follow us in Johnny Quest, our Nissan minivan. As we drove, my brothers-in-law sang "Oklahoma!" repeatedly until

PAPER CHASE

we reached Oklahoma City. I was so happy to arrive that I could finally enjoy some peace! I was even more thrilled when I saw the sign that read "Welcome to Tennessee." I screamed "Hallelujah!" for getting there safely. Keith probably fell asleep a hundred times during the drive, but was too stubborn to let me take over. He even threatened to punch me if I asked him if he was awake again.

Being in Memphis was intimidating since I didn't know anyone, but I was confident in my ability to navigate a city. I had a sort of built-in compass from being "The Driver" all those years. Corn-fed brothers surrounded me on both sides, all educated and clearly fond of "thick" sistas—if you know what I mean. Whew! I was in heaven; someone help me, Je...sus! As a loyal person, I didn't think looking around would hurt, but I felt guilty for the thoughts I had while doing so.

The leasing agent at our new apartment was a sister named Tangy Williams. I could hardly understand her strong Southern accent, but Tangy was so animated and hilarious that we immediately connected. I didn't connect with everyone, but it felt like God placed her there to befriend me and help me through the challenges ahead.

I was off and running, ready to either sink or swim and make some money. I began searching for a job, while my partner, Keith, had already transferred and was set. Each morning, I would turn my compass on and take the children with me to learn my way around, find childcare, and secure employment. Even while managing the kids, I had to fend off unwelcome attention from local men. Did I have "new meat" stamped on my forehead?

I found an in-home daycare outside of Germantown, a suburb of Memphis. The daycare provider, Becky, was Southern Baptist and the whitest person I had ever seen. Luckily, she was flexible with hours, allowing me the freedom to work. Eventually, I landed a job at FedEx as a customer service representative. At that time, FedEx was considered one of the best companies to work for in Memphis.

PAPER CHASE

However, it felt like I was back on the roller coaster of abuse. Whether I took too long at the grocery store or was delayed coming home from work, Keith seemed to find any excuse to hit me. I began to think he would use any pretext to hurt me, and I wondered if he secretly hated women because of his brutality. Why didn't his family warn me that this wasn't unusual behavior for him? Apparently, it was in his bloodline. With no one to talk to, I started confiding in my supervisor, Phyllis Cook. Phyllis loved to cook and often brought in her latest culinary creations for the team to try.

One evening, Tangy came by the apartment with a maintenance man to make some repairs and noticed the bruises on my face. She shared that she had been in an abusive relationship that she was able to escape from, thanks to God. She then asked me, "What would your grandmother say?" I was puzzled by the question, but it made me think: Big Momma would definitely not approve of me allowing anyone to treat me this way. Tangy and I became good friends; in fact, I often used her home as a refuge on late nights when I was fleeing from the beatings. Later, I learned that the family structure in the South was different; grandmothers served as matriarchs, and it was important to make them proud.

Keith started staying out late after work, often coming home too tired to argue or engage in anything else. I felt relieved, as he reminded me of the monster he could be, and I could never shake that feeling. Despite having five children, I had not enjoyed conceiving any of them. I believed "Break Up to Make Up" was his secret theme song. Although I appreciated not having to interact with Keith as much, I was becoming lonely and felt disrespected. I continued to pray, asking God to protect me and the children and to bless our marriage.

However, nightmares began to plague me. Each night, I felt the weight of depression pulling me down a dark path I had never traveled before. I lived in fear and often imagined myself in a casket

PAPER CHASE

during my dreams. I questioned why God allowed me to endure so much pain.

PAPER CHASE

CHAPTER NINE

The day I met Darrel Womack, I was grocery shopping at the Piggly Wiggly, barely able to stop crying for more than ten minutes at a time. Darrel asked me how I was doing, and I replied, "I'm fine." He gently touched the side of my face, where there was a dried tear, and said, "Everything will be okay, baby girl." Darrel gave me his business card and invited me to a fitness club where he worked as a personal trainer. I later learned he was a former Minnesota Vikings player.

Meanwhile, Keith received a call from Child Protective Services about his two children, Lil Keith and his daughter. Apparently, their mother had abandoned them at a stranger's house. I found out she had also been brutally abused by Keith and coped with that abuse by using crack.

We needed to take the kids in, but a full home study had to be completed first. We should have won an Academy Award for the performance we put on for those people. The report they wrote about our home, neighborhood, and family dynamics depicted a perfect marriage and home life. Keith and his father drove to Indiana to get the children. I hate to sound selfish, but wasn't I already dealing with enough? I wasn't happy about the situation, but knowing that the kids had no one else, I stepped up and became a mom to them.

Several months passed, and I found myself occasionally looking at Darrel's business card when I felt depressed. I often thought about how he had approached me and how he had made me feel during one of the lowest emotional points in my life. That thought was uplifting. Finally, one day, I decided to call him, and he again invited me to come to the club to work out. When I arrived at the club, he met me in the parking lot, opened my car door, and said, "What took you so long to call me, baby girl?" Up to that point, Darrel was the finest man I had ever met in person. He was 6 feet tall, weighed 170 pounds of muscle, had caramel-colored

PAPER CHASE

skin, light brown eyes, soft, wavy hair, and smooth skin. I often wondered what Darrel saw in me.

Keith claimed to be working all the time, which I knew was a lie. At this point, I didn't care what Keith did, as long as he left me alone. That gave me a much-needed break from the beatings and the cruel words; I was finally free to go to the health club whenever I wanted. Tangy would watch the kids, and I went to the club at least four times a week. My already strong figure began to look even better. Without an ounce of fat on my body, I had never felt so good physically in my life. The problem was that I still felt broken and sad in my heart, which led to low self-esteem. There were no issues with bills or money, which meant we could do just about whatever we wanted. Soon, we moved out of the apartment and into a beautiful home in Germantown, near the childcare center. Germantown was a prominent area outside of Memphis. Our house was fantastic, featuring a huge kitchen, spacious closets, hardwood floors, and a large yard on the eighth hole of a golf course. We

PAPER CHASE

bought all new furniture and appliances; the sky was the limit, and I picked out whatever I wanted. I decorated each room with different themes: antique for the formal living room, contemporary for the family room, and country style for the kitchen, complete with a pine table and coordinated bench seats. It was amazing! Our home could have been featured in any décor magazine. I kept everything so clean that it looked as if it were a model home, and it didn't seem like small children even lived there. Visitors would often say, "It doesn't look like anyone even lives here." I took lots of pictures for my mom and shared some with Darrel.

Darrel and I began to grow closer. We enjoyed long lunches and walks in the park along the Mississippi River. He would look at me as if he were gazing into my soul, telling me how beautiful I was and complimenting my skin. He loved seeing me in jeans and probably bought me a new pair each week as a gift. On Sundays, I would sneak away to ride on the back of his motorcycle to popular cruising spots; the bike scene was a big

PAPER CHASE

part of life in Memphis. Darrel began to express his desire for me to leave Keith, assuring me he would take care of the children and me. I was surprised because, despite feeling good about myself physically, I thought Darrel was out of my league. He was nice, appeared to be a good father to his twin boys, and he was wealthy!

Darrel understood that I didn't yet trust him enough to move in together, so he didn't pressure me. Our lunches soon moved to his home in Germantown, not far from where I lived. His part of Germantown featured larger, beautiful colonial-style homes with four-car garages and housekeepers. Although Darrel and I had not had sex, he was becoming impatient and started calling my house more frequently. "Hey, Baby girl," he would say, sometimes catching Keith at home, which raised Keith's suspicions about what I had been doing while he was off doing his own thing. I loved the song, "Who's making love to your old lady while you are out making love?"

PAPER CHASE

Keith began to stay home more often, and I wondered what was happening at work. However, since money was never an issue, I didn't investigate. Whenever he did go to work, he would come straight home afterward. Around this time, I noticed his paycheck had dropped significantly. Deciding to take a seasonal job at a department store for extra Christmas money and to get some distance from Keith, I faced his fury. He didn't want me to work, but I stood up for myself, even if it meant getting a black eye. By then, I had learned to take a punch, but I also started fighting back. The fights became more violent, but at least it wasn't easy for him anymore. I figured he would think twice from then on.

I shared my plans with Darrel, and he was thrilled. He remarked, "Perfect! We can finally spend more time together." Darrel even offered to pay me each week and asked me not to go to work, just to come to his house instead. I thought about it and decided I wanted to earn that extra money on my own. Times were getting tight, but not because our

PAPER CHASE

income had decreased; expenses had increased with the additional kids. I expected Keith's paycheck to shrink even more soon because he mentioned he had used a lot of vacation time and would have to take unpaid leave due to health problems stemming from his diabetes. I hoped life would serve him consequences; surely he deserved worse than what my great-grandmother experienced.

One night, after a run-in with Keith's fist, I didn't feel like going to work and decided to visit Darrel instead. I called him to let him know I was on my way. When I arrived, I found a note on the door that read, "Hey baby girl, come on in."

As I entered the house, I noticed a trail of rose petals leading to the family room, where I saw a bar set up. On the bar was a large bottle of Cognac, an ice bucket, and a glass. Beaming with excitement, I thought to myself, "This is my drink of choice!" I poured myself a glass and settled onto the luxurious Italian leather sofa. Leaning over to turn on some music, I found another note that said,

PAPER CHASE

"Now that you have your drink and the music on, go into the bathroom." I smiled, thinking, Oh, he thinks he knows me.

When I entered his bathroom—larger than most bedrooms—I was delighted to find a bath waiting for me, scented with fragrances from Victoria's Secret. There were several different lotions, oils, and perfumes laid out. Undressing, I got into the bathtub with my drink in hand while R. Kelly's "TP-2.com" played in the background.

My head was spinning; I had honestly never experienced anything like this before in my life. I had only seen scenes like this in movies! I relaxed in the bathtub for what felt like hours, warming up the water a few times. Once I finally exited the tub and grabbed a towel, another note fell out: "Look in the closet, baby girl."

I found a Guess bag on a chaise lounge chair in the closet. Inside were matching panties and a bra, black Guess jeans, a black and gold Guess fitted T-shirt, and gold high heels. Filled with

PAPER CHASE

excitement, I sat down on the lounge chair to apply my lotion, then quickly put on the panties and bra. On a small table next to the lounge chair, I noticed another bottle of Cognac in an ice bucket, so I poured myself another drink before getting dressed. Darrel seemed to anticipate every move I would make.

As I waited for him, I started to wonder what all this romancing was about. Suddenly, I heard the music change to Musiq Soulchild's "Love." I could hear Darrel singing along. I walked into the family room and there he was—my handsome caramel man, wearing a beater and gym shorts. He greeted me with a long hug, a passionate kiss, and takeout from Neely's Bar-B-Que. After I ate, Darrel went back into the room. When he returned, he looked sharp in a sky-blue linen leisure suit, complete with gold cufflinks, matching gators, and a brimmed hat the same color as the suit. I had never seen him in anything other than gym clothes or jeans.

PAPER CHASE

He extended his hand, and I followed him out. We pulled up to one of the hottest clubs in Memphis. According to the radio and members of Three 6 Mafia, the line to get in stretched two blocks long. Darrel circled the parking lot in his SUV and pulled back up to the front. The enormous security guard greeted him as if he owned the place. A gorgeous hostess escorted us to the VIP section, explaining that the club was extra packed because Three 6 Mafia and Project Pat were scheduled to make an appearance later, as they were back in town for a Thanksgiving concert.

Darrel showed me off as if I were Halle Berry; it felt like a dream. We danced the whole night, laughed, talked, and he introduced me to everyone we encountered as "his" baby girl. We were having a great time when suddenly our eyes locked; it was as if we were held in a trance. Without saying a word, he sent me a message—it was time to leave the club.

We arrived back at Darrel's house, and I felt carefree, the music of R. Kelly still echoing in my mind. As we pulled up, I sang, "Come on and braid my hair." Darrel asked me to grab a bag from the back seat, and I was puzzled about why I hadn't noticed it before. He later confessed that the beautiful hostess at the club had placed it in the truck while we were seated.

Once inside the house, Darrel mentioned there was something comfortable in the bag. I playfully smacked his arm and said he had ruined the surprise. "No, I didn't," he replied. I headed into the bedroom to shower, feeling sweaty from all the dancing.

When I opened the gift bag, I was surprised to find a long, white satin, sexy, see-through nightgown with matching panties, a robe, and slippers. After applying my scented lotion, oil, and perfume, I went to the kitchen, attracted by the aroma of breakfast. Darrel was busy cooking. He must have heard me coming because there was a hot cup of coffee waiting for me at the table.

PAPER CHASE

As he prepared grits, eggs, bacon, and toast, I appreciated his culinary skills, a gift inherited from his Mississippi upbringing. He fixed our plates and sat down across from me. It was almost 4 a.m., and I realized this night would soon come to an end as I had to get out of work at 6.

I thanked Darrel for treating me so special and for making me feel like I was in a movie. Tears filled my eyes as I asked him, "Why me? Why do I deserve this?" He replied that from the first day he met me, he knew I was special. He felt it was his duty to be an example of a true man and mend my broken heart. He came around to my side of the table and told me I should be treated like a queen, assuring me that God had something special planned for my life. We began to kiss, and that night, we made passionate love for the first time. I realized that all my previous experiences had merely been sex; this was genuine love.

PAPER CHASE

I woke up in a panic at 8 a.m. Oh my God, I was supposed to get off at 6! I hurriedly got dressed, stuffed all my gifts into a bag, and rushed home, scrambling to come up with a lie. My hair was a mess; how would I explain that? Then it hit me—I would say I had stopped by Tangy's for coffee, and she helped wrap my hair.

When I entered the house, the TV was on, and the children were up, surprisingly quiet. They greeted me with a chorus of "hi, mom," and my older daughters rushed over to hug me, but their expressions hinted something was wrong—they looked at me as if they had seen a ghost. I proceeded with my lie about visiting Tangy's, but I still could smell Darrel's scent on my skin, making me anxious.

Keith walked into the family room, and I said, "Hey," which was my usual greeting. I explained my stop on the way home, but he didn't respond; he simply turned and walked away.

PAPER CHASE

Keith and I had barely spoken lately; he spent most of his time in the office on the new computer we had purchased. I felt horrible; overwhelming guilt washed over me. My night with Darrel replayed in my mind, making me wonder what it would be like to move in with him, as he had suggested. Three weeks passed, and I continued to avoid seeing Darrel after that unforgettable night. Eventually, he called and asked me to stop by the club to pick up my Christmas gift. I agreed.

As I headed to the club, I felt no excitement about seeing Darrel like I had before. Regardless of his intentions, we both knew our situation was wrong. As usual, he met me in the parking lot, opened my door, and invited me inside. I took his hand and followed him, recalling our passionate night together.

He said he missed me and thought maybe we had rushed things, noting that something had changed, and he sensed I was not satisfied with him. I tried to explain that our relationship felt like adultery, filling me with guilt, even though I wasn't

PAPER CHASE

in love with Keith. I shared that things would be different if I weren't married with children. At that moment, Darrel placed a finger gently over my lips and said, "I have something just for you, Baby girl."

He pulled out a beautifully wrapped small rectangular box that looked like it might contain jewelry. I loved jewelry and usually wore two to three herringbone chains at a time, so I eagerly opened the box. To my surprise, it was a key—a key to his house. Just as I was about to respond, Darrel was called out of the room to assist a client. I left quickly, not even saying goodbye.

On the drive home, I reflected on my dreams of the perfect family—a husband, a wife, kids, a dog, a big house, and two cars. My ideal life felt further away than ever, and I wondered if it was even possible with Keith. Could I love him again? As I stared into the gift box at a red light, I contemplated what might be. "Jesus, please help me," I whispered, tears rolling down my face. What had I gotten myself into? My body and soul craved Darrel, but my heart wouldn't trust him; it didn't

PAPER CHASE

trust any man. I couldn't understand why Darrel wanted me, as he seemed too good, too fine—perhaps even too nice and gentle—for someone like me.

When I got home, Keith was already angry. The sound of our kids playing and laughing only seemed to irritate him more. He started complaining about how I was nothing without him, how he took care of everything. I silently thought, "This motherfucker wouldn't even know how to pay the light bill," because I had always managed our finances. I'm no saint, but I know God, and He loves me, I reminded myself. I needed to make a good decision and use sound judgment this time. Keith hurled hurtful insults—"you ain't shit," "bitch," "whore," and even derided my family. I absorbed each insult in silence, constantly praying for God to help Keith refrain from saying such mean things to me. I didn't know how it would happen, but I told Keith many times that he would eat his words one day.

PAPER CHASE

The next morning, I stayed home because the babysitter—an old-fashioned Southern Baptist—had washed out one of the kids' mouths with soap for saying "shit." My second youngest had simply told the babysitter that the youngest, who still wore diapers, had "shit" in her pants. She didn't know any better; she was just repeating what she had heard us say. I felt ready to confront that woman. When I tell you that I dragged her for at least a block, please believe me—I did just that! I dared her to call the police because I would also press charges against her for abusing my child.

I typically didn't use the computer much at home, but that day I decided to search for a new daycare. Suddenly, an instant message popped up from a screen name, Jasmine: "Can you talk?" Of course, I could talk, so I quickly typed back. We chatted for close to an hour, and my suspicions were confirmed: they had exchanged photos, phone numbers, and sexual fantasies. I left the chat history open on the computer screen as proof. When Keith came home that evening, after using the

PAPER CHASE

restroom and drinking some water, his first stop was the computer. He accused me of invading his privacy and insisted I was wrong. I remained silent the whole time, fearful of being hit, but I kept a miniature wooden bat nearby just in case.

Christmas passed, and the children received everything on their wish lists. I cooked a fantastic dinner and took lots of pictures for my mom. Darrel met me down the street to pick up his plate; I couldn't deprive him of my cooking—he loved it. In 1999, we all had a great day watching movies, playing cards, and dominoes. Tangy and her boys came by to exchange gifts, but left quickly; Keith never liked any of my friends, creating an atmosphere of tension whenever they visited.

There was so much hype about 1999, with predictions that the year 2000 could mean the end of time. I began to seek God's guidance regarding my choices and my recent interactions with Darrel. I figured even if humanity was spared and we all entered the year 2000 safely, I wanted my heart to be right with God. So, I asked for forgiveness for my sins and prayed for my family. It had to be done. No matter how nice or how good-looking Darrel was, he was not my husband.

I called Darrel and asked him to meet me at the gas station near my house on Germantown Road. When I met him, I told him we had to break it off because I wanted God to bless my marriage, and I returned his key. Darrel looked shaken and surprised; he didn't say a word, just stared at me with an ice-cold gaze before getting into his SUV and driving away. I cried like a baby as Darrel, my dream guy, left me forever.

On December 28th, 1999, we headed to the grocery warehouse. We stocked up on tons of water, beans, peanut butter, flashlights, candles, and any non-perishable items we could find. Everyone was in a frenzy, preparing for what many believed was the end of the world. Some people even bought generators while we prayed for safety. I kept reminding myself of the Bible scripture that says, "No man knows the day or hour."

PAPER CHASE

On New Year's Eve, we enjoyed our traditional finger foods, apple cider, and champagne at home—our "Zoo Zoo's and Wham Wham's," as we called them. At around 11:50 PM, we sat close together, as if we were bracing for an explosion. We opened our eyes at 12:02 AM, relieved to find that we were still safe. I couldn't help but think, "What are we going to do with all this water and peanut butter?" and felt a bit foolish.

During that time, diabetes was becoming an epidemic. Keith's mother was becoming very ill from complications related to the disease. The local phone companies started offering long-distance services, which rendered the company that Keith worked for obsolete. We decided to move to Illinois to be closer to his mother. Deven, Keith's brother—whom I had met years earlier after his release from prison—came down to help us with the move. Devin was a good person and did not condone physical abuse. He had a sassy, intelligent girlfriend named Margie, who Keith's mother adored and spoke highly of. Margie found us a wonderful colonial-style

PAPER CHASE

house. Since we had some savings, I didn't have to worry about finding a job right away.

Many days, I daydreamed about Darrel and what could have been. I missed my beautiful house and felt uncertain about what lay ahead in Illinois. I also thought about Tangy and what a good friend she had been. Finally, we loaded up and said goodbye to Memphis, Tennessee.

PAPER CHASE

CHAPTER TEN

The drive to Illinois was only six hours, significantly shorter than the drive to Memphis from Arizona. We pulled up on the scene in no time. We pulled up in front of the house, Margie found us, and my eyes could not believe what they were seeing. It was horrible! It looked like Eddie Munster's house; you know the one from the Munsters' television show. It stunk of mildew, the roof had been leaking, and a 2000-pound tree had fallen in the yard, damaging the back patio. The attic was full of the old tenant's things, mostly junk. The basement was like a dungeon and had been an old coal mine. What the hell? I was furious! How can anyone believe that I would be okay with living in this dump, knowing what I am accustomed to?

Monica was one of the first relatives I met; her nickname was "Maniac"! She partied like a rock star, even on Sundays. She was good people and very perceptive—she knew what Keith was doing to me without me even having to tell her. Monica gave me my first book, which was a self-help book called "In the Meantime." I loved Monica like a sister right away. She always said, "Cuz, I love you more, huh?" adding "huh?" at the end of her statement as if I had asked her a question. She made me smile.

I was in for the challenge of a lifetime with this house, determined to make it livable. The overhaul began; I cleaned the house from top to bottom and bottom to top. No matter how much Pine-Sol I used, the house still smelled like mildew. I decorated it nicely with all the new things we had purchased in Memphis. Our Golden Retriever, Jasper, was in an uproar and began scratching at the tile on the dining room floor. Soon after, Keith made us put him in what we called "The Dungeon."

As time passed, the house became livable, and the smell started to fade, but the huge tree in the backyard remained. The slumlord landlord sent someone to chop it up, but they never hauled it away. No matter how much I cleaned and tried to make this house a home, I hated it and was sure it was haunted.

Two houses down, a nicely manicured home went up for sale. This house was perfect; it had five bedrooms and was completely remodeled. After two days of negotiation, we purchased this home and moved our belongings down the block by the next weekend. It was the cutest country-style home, and it even had a place for a garden.

I began attending the family church with my children because there wasn't much else I could do. Keith believed that friends were a threat to him. "I'm a lady," I would tell him; I would never betray his friends. My life revolved around home, work, church, and the grocery store. I still didn't have any friends like other people did. However, the older ladies at the church took a liking to me, and Keith's mother adored me, so they became my friends.

As Mamma Violet's health began to deteriorate, I witnessed the terrible effects of the disease that plagued her, eating away at her limbs

PAPER CHASE

like it had done to my great-grandmother Henrietta in the past. The fighting between Keith and me slowed down significantly, though I couldn't tell if it was because Keith didn't want to worry Violet or if he was just too exhausted from his 130-mile round-trip commute to work in the city.

On a typical Tuesday after a holiday, the bank was extremely busy. While processing transactions, I received a phone call informing me that Mamma Violet was being transported to a better hospital in St. Louis. I left work early that day and headed over with Keith and other family members. We stayed all night and drove back home, which was 70 miles one way. The following morning, we woke up early and returned to the hospital. I will never forget that day as long as I live.

We waited patiently in the waiting room and took turns visiting her in the ICU. She was in so much pain from her kidneys shutting down and kept apologizing for leaving us. She knew she was dying. A few hours later, she passed away, and I was right there with her. She will always live on in my heart.

PAPER CHASE

The day of the funeral, it rained heavily, creating a muddy mess at the cemetery.

After Violet's death, my life took another downward turn, and things quickly spiraled out of control. I had grown tired of the abuse and knew I deserved better, so I started to fight back even harder. Although I had been defending myself for a while, I was usually overpowered each time. I figured that my resistance only made the beatings worse, but he bore scars too. I started grabbing anything I could find— a hammer, a knife, a box cutter, an iron— it didn't matter. This made my life dangerously volatile; with all the violence, either of us could have killed the other at any moment.

To complicate matters, Keith's constant suspicion revolved around whether or not I was cheating, which I wasn't—unless you could consider "prayer" cheating, but it certainly wasn't being answered. My older children wanted to visit their father, Lavelle, who was now stationed in Maryland. He drove down to pick them up along with his new wife and baby. While I was happy for him, he still harbored resentment toward me.

After the girls left with Lavelle, they must have filled him in on all the drama, because the next thing I knew, a process server handed me legal documents. Lavelle was suing for full custody of the girls, claiming that they had been abused. My heart felt like it was being ripped from my chest again. My children wouldn't even speak to me, and because of their statements, a full child protective services (CPS) investigation was launched to look into Keith's treatment of the kids, which included Lil Keith, his sister, my son, and the two daughters Keith and I shared. After a month of CPS visits and court appearances, I was no longer in jeopardy of losing my other children. However, my oldest daughters still wouldn't talk to me. Lavelle had put them both on anti-depressant medication, claiming that their emotional problems were all my fault—that I had chosen Keith over my kids.

PAPER CHASE

Keith was now depressed because he missed his mother and was also taking anti-depressant medication. After crashing his vehicle head-on into a house one afternoon in an attempt to end his life, Keith thought it best for us to move back to Arizona. He took a position at his brother's firm, which ran a very successful consulting business in the automobile industry. For nine months, Keith commuted back and forth between Arizona and Illinois. Finally, in November 2003, during the week of Thanksgiving, we began loading up the truck to move back.

Monica, Keith's cousin, cooked Thanksgiving dinner for us and reminded me, "Cuz, I love you more, huh?" She told me to find her a house because she was planning to come to Arizona too. The day after Thanksgiving, we headed for the sunshine just as the snow began to fall. It was a long drive. By the time we reached New Mexico, we could see the smoke from the forest fires burning in Northern Arizona. Finally, we saw a sign that read "Welcome to Scottsdale," and all I could think about

PAPER CHASE

was seeing my mother. However, Keith insisted that we stop at his brother's house first. He worked for his brother and hadn't seen him in years, and since their family was well-off, they had visited Illinois several times. I was furious; I hadn't seen my mother in over five years.

Finally, we got the okay to leave, and we argued about whether we were going to my mom's. "Oh, we're going," I said, and I bet that was exactly where we ended up. When my mom came out of the house, I couldn't believe my eyes. She could barely walk; her whole left side was stiff, and her face looked as though a monster had overtaken one side of it. I begged for an explanation. "What happened?" I asked. She explained that she had suffered a stroke that affected the left side of her body and caused Bell's palsy, which impacted her facial muscles. We said our goodbyes and then headed toward our new home.

Keith rented a home in a prominent area of the city, often referred to as "Baller, Shot Caller Status." It was stunning, featuring 20-foot vaulted ceilings, a tile entryway adorned with a medallion, an office, a living room, an Arizona room, and a huge kitchen equipped with top-of-the-line appliances. There were five spacious rooms upstairs, and the master bedroom even included a Jacuzzi. Keith had already furnished the place with new items he purchased as a surprise, and his choices reflected my own taste well.

Back to reality. I planned to return to the bank while Keith worked for his brother's firm. My family kept their distance because they disapproved of how Keith treated me. Monica had arrived to look for a new place, and I had several options lined up for her to consider. She chose a house and wanted to celebrate, so Keith and I took her to a local spot known as the "Hole in the Wall."

Once there, we had a great time. I encountered many familiar faces from high school and greeted both men and women alike.

PAPER CHASE

Somehow, I had forgotten who I was married to. Suddenly, I was yanked out of the club and thrown onto the ground as if I were nothing. I blacked out for a moment, removed my 8-inch wedge heels, and decided to give Keith a taste of his own medicine. I chased him all the way to the car, which was at least 60 feet away. I was fed up with his behavior. When I say he received a serious beating that night, I mean it!

I spent the night at my sister's house and moved out of that beautiful home the next morning, taking all the children with me except for Lil Keith, who had been having some behavioral problems. Earlier that month, the toilet in the master bedroom had broken, so I had to walk to the kids' restroom late one night. As I passed the room where Lil Keith and my son were sleeping, I heard some commotion. I opened the door and what I saw filled me with fear and anger. My son's pants were down, and Lil Keith was on top of him, seemingly trying to assault him.

My son was crying and trembling with fear. I screamed, waking everyone in the house. I grabbed my son, hugged him tightly, and cried so hard I thought I might convulse.

Keith called the police to report what had happened, and we were all taken to what the police referred to as the Child Help Center. We were questioned, and my son received a physical examination. Thank God he had not been penetrated; he wasn't raped.

So many emotions swirled through my mind. Why can't my life go right? Why does it feel like the devil is constantly trying to remind me of my childhood traumas, with a monster lurking in various forms? Why can't the man I call my husband treat me properly? I want to love only him, but he is so cruel. I continuously think about ways to escape from him. Deep down, I know I should have stayed with Darrel back in Memphis.

Staying in one small bedroom with all my children is becoming increasingly challenging after a month. Recently, it was Lil Keith's birthday, and I took the children to celebrate with him. Even

PAPER CHASE

though Lil Keith had attempted to harm my son, I still loved him and felt sympathy for him because he had been a victim of a similar incident in the past. While his mother was involved with someone on Hyades, he was molested by one of her so-called boyfriends. I insisted that he undergo counseling before I would allow him to be around the other children again. Somehow, Keith managed to convince me to stay at the celebration. I couldn't help but wonder what my sister would think. I knew she would be furious, especially since she had helped pick the gravel out of my legs and buttocks from a previous incident. Despite staying for the celebration, I had reached my limit. "God, please help me," I cried out in desperation.

One day, Keith found a door hanger advertising a local church, and we decided to visit. The church was filled with smiling faces, and they emphasized family and marriage while teaching a message of prosperity. One woman stood out to me—a white lady named Clara, the only white person there. She approached us and said that God wanted her to speak with us before we left. The things she shared with Keith and me resonated deeply and encouraged us to keep coming back. Clara told me that she knew I had been hurt badly over the years and that God had told her to let me know it was time to be free.

I had been tormented for years by the memories of the molestation and rape I suffered as a child. I was exhausted from the pain those memories brought back. One Sunday morning, I lay at the altar and surrendered all my worries to God. I left behind the unforgiveness I had carried for years regarding my childhood. Eventually, we joined the church and became very active in its ministry, even enrolling in the Bible college there. For two straight years, Keith did not lay a hand on me; things had truly changed.

So here we are again, trying to make this marriage be what it's supposed to be, and I have never been more in love. Things had never been better. Keith had become a different person in many ways. He had control of his temper, and he was

PAPER CHASE

working in the ministry, feeding the homeless, and fundraising. Thank you, Jesus, He treated me like a queen, opening car doors, buying gifts, telling me how beautiful I was. Wow! I was so thankful. In return, I was the best wife I could be by doing all the "wifely things" - you know, cooking, cleaning, and managing the money and bills. We were in a good place.

I began to cater more and more to upscale clients, and the list of doctors, entertainers, and politicians was amazing. I did all this while working for a very large financial institution that paid me very well. Keith was in advertising, so he helped with the marketing aspect of my business. I began to get better and better at my God-given gift, cooking. The calls continued coming in from word of mouth and advertising. I barely slept from all the new business. Big Momma would be so proud of me.

Soon, we saved enough money to purchase a home, our first mini-mansion. And you can best believe, no expense was spared. We installed everything from new appliances, carpet, tile, to custom paint. Right before closing on our loan, Keith wanted to talk to me. I thought Oh boy, he looks worried. I prayed to God, Please don't let anything be wrong with him. Diabetes had become quite the nuisance and was taking him through a lot of physical changes. We sat down, he looked into my eyes and told me how much he loved me, what a great wife I was, and how he would never love anyone else. Then he told me he had been unfaithful several months earlier and had conceived a child. My heart was being slowly cut from my body with a sharp scalpel, with no pain medicine. Once my heart fell onto the floor, it was pissed on. *What the hell did I ever do to deserve this treatment? Was this payback for my relationship with Darrell back in Memphis?*

Shortly after moving into our new home, Keith was laid off from his advertising job and began working for his oldest brother again. The economy had taken a turn for the worse, and if something was not absolutely necessary, people

PAPER CHASE

weren't buying it. As a result, advertising was no longer as important to business owners.

I wanted to distance myself from Keith as much as possible, so I took the long way home each day. Lil Keith continued to display inappropriate sexual behavior, which forced me to stay up all night, monitoring him and ensuring the safety of the other children. I was exhausted and frustrated; I loved him, but I knew he had to go. Eventually, we sent Lil Keith back to his mother, who had resurfaced and claimed to be clean from drugs.

I began to focus on growing my catering business and helping my mother, who was now very sick due to diabetes. This disease was driving me crazy. Why did it feel like some sort of limb-eating demon? I completely ignored the disappointment I felt towards this man. I thought it was time to pull it together and see things for what they really were. Nobody is perfect, and he was honest by confessing his struggles. I decided it was time to discuss it with him. I firmly believed that a man needs to take care of his children, and I expected Keith to do the

PAPER CHASE

right thing for this child who didn't ask to come into this world. Keith told me that he wanted nothing to do with the child, claiming it served as a reminder of the horrible mistake he had made. How could he turn his back on his child? Who does that?

Then, the phone rang; it was my sister, Stephanie. She explained that our mother had suffered a stroke and urged me to get to the hospital right away. I rushed out of the house as if someone had set me on fire. When I arrived at the hospital, it felt like I was in a low-budget horror film. This couldn't be happening, not to my mom, I thought to myself. My sister had a blank expression on her face as I entered the waiting area and said the doctor would be out shortly.

"Sharon West family," the doctor announced as he approached us. We gathered around him, anxious for news. He informed us that she was out of danger; the stroke had caused Bell's palsy, which affected her speech and slightly deformed her face, but she would survive.

PAPER CHASE

I was extremely busy, but I had to figure out a way to help my Mom. She would have to move in with me; this was the second time she had suffered a stroke. I began to pack up her place. Her new husband was nowhere to be found, and Candy, the baby my Auntie Joan had, was in foster care. Apparently, my Mom and her husband had been separated when I lived in Illinois because of his daughter punching my mother. I'm still looking for that bitch. I'm throwing half of my Mom's shit away because it's older than Abraham Lincoln, and the rest is going into storage. Mom had her own room and bathroom in the west wing of our home. She was getting better, recovering from the stroke miraculously. The Bell's palsy was leaving and her speech was returning. I barely even remember Keith being around when all this was going on. I guess it is fair to assume I was completely consumed with being a daughter, mother, businesswoman, and caretaker.

I remember the long conversations we had. There were many aspects of her choices that I didn't understand. I asked her about her childhood and why she stayed with the mean Midwesterner, Curtis, for so long. She explained that she always needed stability, and that's what he provided for her. "Things were different in my day," she said, as if to justify the way men treated women. A little voice in my head said, "Bullshit." I just smiled at my mom. She also mentioned that she was 100% sure two of Auntie June's kids were fathered by Curtis. I thought to myself, that's why they favored him so much; it wasn't because she "marked them." I'll be damned. She continued reminiscing about her brothers and sisters, and how they would play and climb trees. All of a sudden, my mom started to cry and became very upset. I didn't know how to react. I thought that talking about her childhood made her think of Big Momma. I held my mom in my arms as if she were a small child, trying to comfort her. All of a sudden, as she wept, she said, "He raped him, he raped my brother". I damn near dropped her on the floor and rose to my feet. I asked my mom, What are you talking about? Clarence, Clarence raped Isaiah, she said. I was speechless and I could not say a word. Everything in my gut said this is what unc was going to tell me that day at Latrice's house before he died. That was the demon that he had wrestled with his whole life, which is what drove him to a life of crime and drugs. God help Clarence's soul.

My mother was finally well enough to live on her own, so we applied for her SSI Disability benefits. This meant we needed to find a place that offered subsidized housing since she was on a fixed income. The search began. My mom was used to living in a prominent neighborhood, so finding a suitable place proved challenging. Typically, subsidized housing is located in less desirable areas, and I wanted to ensure she felt safe in her new home.

After months of searching, we finally hit the jackpot. We found a redeveloped area with brand-new senior living housing that offered subsidized rent. We were thrilled! She got approved, moved in, and settled down, and my mom was so happy to

PAPER CHASE

have a place of her own—a first in her life, as there had always been a man in the picture before.

For a while, I managed all her finances until she learned how to do it on her own. Unlike me, her previous husbands had always handled the finances, so she didn't have experience managing bills or payments.

I needed to take a day off; I was completely worn out, both mentally and physically. So, I called in sick to my 9 to 5 job. During that time, I decided to reach out to my oldest children, who now lived in Japan with Lavelle and his wife. There was definitely some bad blood between us. I felt as though they had turned against me for a white woman. Because of my relationship with Keith, my daughters hadn't spoken to me in years. It hurt that they blamed me for all their pain. You know, it was my fault to some extent. I didn't have to endure all the physical abuse that I did.

While I was searching for the country code to call my children in Japan, I came across some

PAPER CHASE

information stored in my computer that I wished I hadn't seen. Nevertheless, I called my oldest children that day, and they were so happy to hear from me. I missed them so much, and my oldest daughter told me that she wanted to come home. I agreed immediately and started working with Lavelle to purchase her a ticket and bring her back home. I was excited but worried that there would be drama—the same drama that had caused them to leave Illinois.

My daughters mentioned that they were still on their medication. Apparently, everyone in their household was on antidepressants—even the dog. I'm serious; the dog was on Prozac.

PAPER CHASE

CHAPTER ELEVEN

Keith was up to his old tricks again. Was it my fault for being so consumed with my mom? Absolutely not. This wasn't on me; he wasn't worth the ground he walked on. I emailed him at work to let him know that I had discovered his online sexual indiscretions. Honestly, I wondered if I was married to a pervert. Maybe he was one of those monsters. There were girl after girl, naked picture after naked picture, and inappropriate conversation after inappropriate conversation. Tears streamed down my face like Niagara Falls, and my heart was still shattered from the last bout of disrespect. When the kids came home from school, I pulled myself together.

I couldn't help but question them about whether anyone had ever touched them inappropriately. They stared at me with blank faces, offering no response. More tears welled up inside me. I screamed, "ANSWER ME! Has anyone ever touched you inappropriately? Your body is YOUR body!" They replied, "Mom, what's wrong with you? No one has hurt us; calm down."

I went a whole week barely speaking to Keith because I was disgusted. The following Monday, he came home looking like he had seen a ghost. The football game was on, but he went straight into the bedroom and closed the door. That was unusual; he was usually a radical football fan, yelling and cursing at the television. Some days he cursed so much that I thought the TV might go on strike. I assumed he had received more bad news about his health since he had a doctor's appointment that morning. The medications he was taking caused him to have erectile dysfunction, which was fine by me because I had no interest in sex with anyone.

Finally, he emerged from the bedroom and asked, "Can I talk to you?" He then said, "I got suspended from work for a few days without pay, all because of a misunderstanding."

PAPER CHASE

"WHAT? With a new mortgage? What happened?" I asked.

A woman is claiming that I sexually harassed her. My mouth dropped open as feelings of humiliation churned in my stomach. My heart was already heavy; I felt completely unaffected after a few hours, which is a dangerous state to be in. Strong women know what I'm saying: when you've been hurt so badly that you become numb, your reactions can be unpredictable.

He admitted to flirting with her, but nothing more. The following morning, his brother called me to explain the entire situation. Keith had been going to lunch with this woman and meeting her in the parking lot for hours after work. Everyone at the company knew they were involved. When the woman decided she had had enough—perhaps because he couldn't perform—she called it off, and he attempted to demote her. What an idiot to jeopardize his brother's business for a fling; if that isn't biting the hand that feeds you, I don't know what is.

PAPER CHASE

Once the dust settled, Keith's brother's company settled out of court with the woman for $50,000, and Keith was fired. I was making good money, but it wasn't enough to maintain our lifestyle and cover a $3,000 a month mortgage on my own. Things were getting ugly, and I often fantasized about burying him in the desert. The only thing that stopped me was the love I have for his family and how they would feel about it.

I made every effort possible, but after six months of steady grinding, the house went into foreclosure. How could everything we worked so hard for be lost over something so trivial? Keith found another job that didn't pay as well, but it was a job nonetheless. We began looking for rentals and moved into a nice house on the golf course, owned by a friendly Hispanic man named Miguel. Miguel's gaze felt intense as we spoke, and he kept insisting that I could call him if we ever needed anything. While Miguel was nice, there was an underlying feeling that he might have been a bit of a dirty old

PAPER CHASE

man, likely interested in a little extra than just collecting rent.

Some of our neighbors on the golf course frequently hosted gatherings, so I was fortunate to fit right into their plans. One year, I organized a Christmas party for some local rappers. When my team and I arrived at the event, I was brought to a screeching halt as soon as I walked in. Something was wrong! There was a man at the party whom I had never seen before, but I instinctively knew he was my biological father. I thought, Am I going crazy? I had never even seen a picture of him or witnessed him visiting Rochelle's house, my childhood neighbor and friend, yet I absolutely knew it was him. My heart raced with a mix of confusion, joy, and anger all at once.

I rushed outside, and my assistant followed me, asking what was wrong. I exclaimed, "That is my father in there!" as tears streamed down my face, feeling as though they were bursting like water balloons on the ground. My assistant, being the inquisitive person she was, went back inside to

PAPER CHASE

investigate. The next thing I knew, this man, who felt like a mirror image of me, came running out of the house, shouting my name as if he had been searching for me all his life. He apologized and expressed his desire to be part of my life. I accepted his apology and chose not to hold the past against him. We talked, laughed, and cried together. It turned out he was a chef.

That night, I met six of my sisters, my grandmother, several aunts and uncles, and about a hundred cousins—all of whom embraced me with open arms. It felt like a miracle. I thought to myself, Good things are going to happen, and this proves it. I desperately needed some family support. On my mom's side of the family, I was always the one everyone leaned on, so I was thrilled to get to know my newfound family. There were constant cookouts and parties. Honestly, my dad would use any excuse to fire up the grill: the Phoenix Suns won a game—a cookout; my nephew graduated from preschool—a cookout; I painted my house—a cookout! They even had a full bar and a tip jar at the parties.

PAPER CHASE

These people were unique. They seemed close-knit, with little drama among them, and they loved to dance. True story: these folks would do the electric slide at a funeral—not at the repast, but right at the funeral. To say the least, they adored enjoying each other's company and eating together. I got to know my sisters, each of whom had young children. Soon, I became the designated babysitter. At first, I didn't mind babysitting because I wanted to bond with my nieces and nephews. They would go out and have fun, sharing their experiences with me later, but eventually, I began to feel used. I asked them, "Why don't you ever invite me?" They responded, "Who's going to babysit?"

My heart ached to get to know these people better, but I felt like I was always the giver and had nothing left to offer. I was starved for healthy family interactions as it was. I had to dedicate more and more time to developing my business, which left me with hardly any time to babysit. The less I babysat, the less I saw my sisters.

PAPER CHASE

However, I became close with one of my dad's sisters, Donna. She loved to cook and was always eager to help me cater events. She is the only person in the world who can make macaroni and cheese better than I can! Donna loved to entertain and had a fantastic sense of style.

At one of my sister's weddings, she arrived wearing a royal purple dress and a matching royal purple wig. And guess what? She totally owned that look! She looked incredible, and not many people could have pulled that off.

In November 2008, during the United States presidential election, I woke up bright and early on the morning of November 4th to head to the polls before work. I had to park six blocks away from the polling place. People had brought lawn chairs, coolers filled with food and drinks, and even grills. Celebrating like it was a tailgate party, individuals from African American, Hispanic, and Caucasian backgrounds were filled with excitement. People with disabilities were rolling themselves in wheelchairs, and caretakers brought those who needed assistance, including oxygen machines. It was an incredible sight to witness. I joined in the celebration, fully aware that I was part of history in the making. Democrat Barack Obama, then a junior United States Senator from Illinois, defeated Republican John McCain, the senior U.S. Senator from Arizona. We now had our first African American president; indeed, nothing is impossible!

At that moment, I realized I had to ramp up my efforts to generate more catering business. I still had a solid job in Corporate America and was networking with influential people: pastors, district attorneys, football players, and many more. One woman I met changed my life forever. She was the main litigant in the largest class action lawsuit in U.S. history. Helen took me under her wing and shared her knowledge about money, business, and love. I hung on to every word as if they were the most important secrets. As it turned out, she owned a restaurant that wasn't doing well, so I began renting her kitchen for my catering events. Before long, I was operating her restaurant on weekends, managing the kitchen while she kept the revenue from the bar. In just two months, I had profited $60,000. It was on!

Soon, I had enough money to rent a suite in a shopping center for my own restaurant, with the help of Keith's oldest brother, who was my number one cheerleader at the time. I paid cash for everything, and things progressed so quickly that there weren't enough hours in the day. I decided to take a leave of absence from my regular job.

Then came the grand opening day! The house was packed—what a sight! Everyone was excited. Our pastor and his wife led the prayer, while our councilman turned the sign to "Open." I imagined my grandmother dancing in heaven, filled with joy. There was a line nearly around the block all day long. One local entrepreneur even offered to showcase his classic cars for a mini car show. A DJ was spinning tunes, and we served complimentary hors d'oeuvres and sparkling cider. I had been working since 6 a.m., and it was now 6 p.m., yet people were still arriving.

PAPER CHASE

I decided to take a quick break before returning to work in the dining room. As I reentered, I greeted guests and checked on their meals, with Keith observing me closely. I didn't think much of it at the time; it was a wonderful day—a mountain had been moved, and we were making progress. I felt so elated that I practically skipped back into the kitchen. My mom, my assistant, and my children were there, and my eldest daughter had even flown in from Japan to visit. I could hardly contain my joy. Suddenly, however, I felt intense pain and struggled to breathe.

Keith had struck me in the head and began to choke me; my life flashed before my eyes. I knew he couldn't get away with hurting me, especially with my family present and guests enjoying their meals. He must have realized he was losing control. Suddenly, he let me go and asked me to come into the office to speak with him. I sat on the floor in disbelief, trying to process what had just happened. It felt as though everyone around me was trying to contain their reactions to spare me the

PAPER CHASE

embarrassment of the guests knowing what occurred. Keith thought I was having an affair with one of the men I had greeted in the dining room. My mom discreetly called the police, which I hadn't done, and asked them to come to the back door of the restaurant. I refused to file a report because I didn't want to involve the police in my business.

Keith quickly jumped into my brand new, customized Yukon XL with Pirelli tires and drove off. I dared him to try to ruin my day. Didn't he realize I didn't need his unhealthy presence in my life? I thought to myself, I was ready to bury the old Stacy and move on. I had my mom drive me to pick up my Cadillac SLS from home so I would have transportation. That same night, I called a car dealership, told them what kind of SUV I needed, and returned to the restaurant with my new truck on 22-inch wheels just three hours later.

The next morning, I was so sore I could barely move. I was embarrassed, and my neck was black and blue. I filed for an order of protection and refused to take his calls. Little did I know that while

PAPER CHASE

I was dealing with the order of protection, he was cleaning out our bank account—$15,000 gone just like that. And there was nothing I could do because I had added him to my account.

Back to business; problems are meant to be solved. I had come too far, and I couldn't stop now. I filed for divorce a week after the incident at the restaurant, ending 11 years of marriage.

A new day arrived, and my children, friends, and even Keith's family cheered me on. My whole life was about to change. I didn't want to remain in the home we shared, which was owned by Miguel, because of the bad memories associated with it. Instead, I found a small, nice rental in the same general area so that the children could continue attending the same school. I was so proud of myself; things were moving along better than ever. The restaurants grossed an average of $1,200 a day. I had a great team and a good support system. My father came by to show his support, and even the grumpy Midwesterner that my mom had married when I was a child frequented my place. Life was good, with no holds barred.

I stayed in close contact with my second-to-oldest daughter, whom I affectionately called "Lil Mama," and Lavelle, who was stationed in Dallas, Texas. As soon as she found out I had finally left Keith, she asked to come home, and I bought her a plane ticket the next day. My daughter had visited for Christmas earlier that year and met a handsome boy at our church. I wasn't convinced that I was the only reason she was coming home; I was pretty sure she wanted to be near this new boy she had met. However, I didn't care why she was coming back—I was just happy to have her back in my life.

No matter how much that horrible man begged me to talk to him, I refused. Did he really think he was God? The kids wanted nothing to do with him either, and even his grandmother told me I should take a stand against him. It was time for some party time and celebration. Tiffany, my loyal friend from the Bay Area, and my good friend Agelique were also single and ready to mingle. The party didn't even start until we arrived; we were definitely turning heads, and few could outdress us. Men were flocking behind us like hungry dogs, which is how I often viewed them. So, we let them buy drinks all night—maybe even breakfast—but they wouldn't get any affection from us.

It might be true that "birds of a feather flock together," because my friends and I always respected our bodies—one-night stands were a big "No." Don't get me wrong; nobody's perfect. There were a couple of indiscretions here and there, but you can bet that: 1. No one else knew, and 2. The guys we met at the club didn't know where we lived—those men never made it home with us.

Those were fun times. Even on nights when Agelique didn't want to go out, I would play T-Pain, singing along and grooving in my seat. I was quite the social butterfly.

When we would arrive at the club, I could only sit down for so long. I would make acquaintances and bring them back to the table with Agelique. I never really understood why I

PAPER CHASE

introduced guys to her when she was super picky about even conversing with someone.

The restaurant continued to thrive, receiving great reviews and landing some catering jobs. My children, my niece, a few cousins, and my friend Agelique all worked with me. Each day was long, but we had fun. Occasionally, my mom would come by and work a few hours; she loved to decorate and clean.

The 2009 NBA All-Star Week was fantastic. Celebrity after celebrity and basketball player after basketball player came in to eat. Some memorable visitors included DJ Drama and Montel Jordan. Both were very down-to-earth; they took pictures and signed autographs. My girl Agelique and I were so tired from cooking that we couldn't even enjoy our VIP status because we were busy soaking our feet.

While shopping at Restaurant Depot earlier this year, I met a guy named James, who seemed really nice. He was from Detroit—"The D," as he called it. Here I was, looking for love in all the

PAPER CHASE

wrong places again, thinking I needed someone else to show me love instead of finding it within myself. The crazy thing is, looking back on all my decisions, I had no idea what love truly was.

James was incredibly handsome, but he was short and looked quite young, even though we were both in our mid-thirties. My friend Agelique and I were living it up; when we weren't working, we were at the club. There seemed to be a different one for every night of the week. The guys would be standing outside, eagerly anticipating our arrival, and the bartenders would have our drinks ready by the time we walked in.

One night, we went out to check out some local talent and unexpectedly ran into James. He followed me around like a dog in heat, and I had no idea he was interested in me in that way. After leaving the club and heading home, my phone began to ring. I fished it out of "The Black Hole" (that's what I called my purse). It was James. He asked, "Where did you go? Come back and hang with me." For real, was this guy actually asking me for some

PAPER CHASE

intimate time? I told him I was headed home and that I didn't know him well enough to go to his place in the middle of the night.

Several weeks passed, and we talked on the phone frequently. I learned a lot about him. He was a gentleman who loved his family, had two boys, loved dogs, and was involved in the rap game. We eventually decided to go on a much-needed dinner date. I laughed so much that I thought I would pass out—this guy was really fun. After our date, we parted ways, and he kissed me on the cheek and said goodnight.

Thanksgiving was a few weeks later, and we decided to spend it together at Agelique's house. The kids were going to go with Keith, so I was free to have company over without them knowing. We kicked it on Thanksgiving, we ate, played cards, drank, and at the end of the night, James pulled me close and gave me a kiss so hot it set my whole body on fire. We continued to talk on the phone and go out. Eventually, it was apparent that each of us wanted to be exclusive. One night after work, he

PAPER CHASE

invited me over to his place for dinner. He cooked the best steak I had ever put in my mouth; his trade was a butcher so he knew his meat cuts. After dinner, we sipped on a Lil Cognac and listened to some of his music from a demo he put together. He could flow; I was so impressed. He made me feel like a young teenager in love. He asked me to come into his bedroom. He had a red light in the lamp so the ambiance was romantic. he burned Nag Champa oil and turned on some TP, If you know you know " I think I better let it go..." He sang along with the music. He whispered in my ear "You should prepare yourself for what I am about to do". Baaaaby I didn't know what to t think, I was like "hold on, I'm not into that freaky shit". My body quivered at his touch. He began to undress me, while caressing my body as he took off my clothes. Each time he touched me, my yoni tingled and pulsated from the anticipation. He left my high heels on and sat me on the bed, he stepped back looking into my eyes intensely and began to undress himself. His body was perfect, smooth, no fat and a six-pack. The waves glistened in his head like he should be on the

PAPER CHASE

cover of GQ magazine. His chocolate skin, perfect teeth and the scent of his body was driving me crazy. Still silent he did not break eye contact with me and reached for some massage oil sitting next to the bed. He told me to lie on my stomach and massaged every inch of my body with so much passion that I could no longer contain myself. I was begging him to be inside me. He started to slowly kiss my yoni; I had never felt this kind of intense pleasure in my life. He licked, sucked and touched my yoni until it was throbbing. My juices were flowing like a river. He climbed on top of me and entered my body so slow that every wonderful thought of our time together began to go through my mind like a slide show. His penis was huge, the pleasure and pain I felt was a new experience. We made love for six hours, I had heard of Gourmet sex, but this was greater than my wildest imagination. I had cum so many times I lost count around 50. I begged him to cum and finally the moment arrived; he came with so much force and passion that we lay stuck together until the next morning. When we woke up we were both weak and needed some nutrition, I could barely walk I was so sore. He told me it was the best sex he ever had in his life. We could not get enough of each other after that; he was my baby and I was his "Honeydew". I introduced him to my mom and my children, everyone loved him and he treated me like a queen. He would cook dinner, help the children with their homework and even run my bath water. This was a fairytale come true, I was deep in love with him and often fantasized about him proposing to me.

PAPER CHASE

CHAPTER TWELVE

By May 2009, business had slowed down tremendously. I had used all my cash to get things started, and my overhead was around $14,000 per month, but I was only making about $600 per day on average. I began to cut back on staff and look for other ways to save money. Repairs and maintenance issues were taking a toll on the budget. First, there was a plumbing problem; waste was literally floating through the restaurant. Then, there was an issue with the grease trap. The AC broke down three times, and the walk-in fridge/freezer malfunctioned as well. All I could do was wonder, "What the hell? I'm using my personal savings, which were meant for household bills, to cover the restaurant expenses."

June 25, 2009, was a strange day. It was nearly 2:00 PM, and we hadn't had a single guest. I was standing there, looking out the window, when I glanced at the television in disbelief. TMZ was reporting that Michael Jackson had died. My phone

PAPER CHASE

began to ring; each call was from a frantic family member telling me to turn on the news. The world changed that day. The economic situation continued to worsen, with rising unemployment and foreclosures reaching an all-time high. If people didn't have a place to live, how could I expect them to eat out? Right before my eyes, everything I had worked so hard for—my life's dream—was being ripped away from me. The restaurant closed in October of that same year. The only thing that helped me keep my sanity about losing my business was the fact that I was incredibly proud of my oldest daughter. She was graduating from high school and had already planned to go straight to veterinary college.

It was time to get back to business. I had no job, no money, and a family to take care of. I knew I could probably find a job; however, the economy and unemployment rate were so bad that I wasn't sure how long it would take. Keith had not contributed a dime to help with the kids. He was a selfish and irresponsible person, and I felt a deep resentment towards him. James, who made good money as a butcher, was practically living with me and rarely went home. He told me not to worry, assuring me that we would get through this together; he made enough money to pay my bills and his.

One late night, while I was relaxing with James, his phone rang. The area code was from his hometown, Detroit. He answered, but quickly dropped the phone to the floor and sat in stunned silence, turning pale as if he were dehydrated. I asked, "What's wrong, baby?" but he still wouldn't say a word. I picked up the phone, and his sister was on the other end. She told me that their grandmother had passed away.

The next morning on the way to the airport, James was still in shock; he barely said two words to me. I waited with him until his flight was ready to board. He looked into my eyes, pulled me close, kissed me, and told me he loved me. He called me when he landed, but I decided to give him space and time to grieve. I only texted him goodnight if we

PAPER CHASE

hadn't spoken. I understood he hadn't seen his boys in a while and probably wanted to spend time with them. He was staying at his sister's house and seemed to be in good spirits, considering the circumstances.

A week had passed, and I was on my way to the airport to pick up James. My mom decided to come over and cook him a welcome-back dinner. I picked him up on the south curb; he got in and greeted me with a sweet kiss, and we headed home. He seemed very tired, ate a bit, and then went upstairs to bed. He appeared a little different, which was to be expected given what he had just gone through.

I had landed a position with another financial institution; things were tight, but my baby had me, so I wasn't worried. On the day James got paid, he handed me $900 and said his check was less than he had anticipated. Something felt off, and a little voice in my head said, "That's probable cause to search his things." I started going through his nightstand drawer and found a check stub for over

PAPER CHASE

$2,000. I thought, What the hell...? He had made his normal pay. I began to feel short of breath.

I was fine if he needed to send money to his two boys, but I wasn't okay with him lying to me. I continued searching his stuff and found a duffel bag in the closet containing his old phone. He had just gotten a new one a week earlier. The phone had text messages from his ex-girlfriend in Detroit, some local girl, and what appeared to be a groupie. He had performed a few shows and had a few groupies following him around. I had never been concerned about other women because I knew where he slept and where his money went.

I discovered letters and cards from his ex-girlfriend in Detroit. The letters discussed how great their sex had been when he was in town for his grandmother's funeral. I became sick to my stomach and ran to the bathroom. Before I could make it to the toilet, I was vomiting and crying all at once. This pain was different. I had been disappointed by Keith for years, but subconsciously, I expected him to disappoint me.

PAPER CHASE

James was different in my eyes. He had swept me off my feet and seemed content with just me. I gathered my wits, got dressed nicely, and headed to pick him up from work. While waiting, I made a respectful phone call to his ex-girlfriend, the mother of one of his sons. I firmly believe in confronting my partner about such matters. I told her who I was and why I was calling; I had read the letters, and they were very upsetting since he had been living with me. She was less than polite and hung up on me. Just then, he was walking to the car; he got in and greeted me as if everything was okay. Did he think I was stupid?

I had the stack of check stubs, pictures, letters, and cards all in one pile. Anger surged through me, and I couldn't control myself. I threw the stack of papers at him as hard as I could and started screaming. "How could you do this to me, James?" He didn't even attempt to explain. We entered the house, and he started packing his things. I hadn't asked him to leave, and deep down,

PAPER CHASE

I didn't want him to. I was willing to give him a second chance; I was just angry.

He refused to talk or argue, and that day he left, not answering my phone calls for weeks. My mom and my kids were devastated as well; they even tried to call him, but he would not respond. When he finally answered my call, he said he still felt responsible for helping me with the bills for a while. He told me to come by his job to get $600 to help with the bills. I was a mess; I hadn't been eating or sleeping and had been drinking too much, but I met him at work. He continued giving me money for three months... I guess until he didn't feel guilty anymore. After that, we never spoke again.

I was still a mess emotionally, but I can tell you one thing: I wasn't planning on getting involved with another man for a long time. I worked crazy hours and was rarely home, and despite my hard work, things were tight financially because catering work was non-existent.

PAPER CHASE

One day, while I was getting gas, a handsome guy caught my eye. It was October 16th, almost my birthday weekend. I must have caught his eye as well because he approached me and introduced himself. I felt embarrassed because my truck smelled like Black and Milds; I had started smoking as a way to cope with my recent breakup with James. The attractive man from South Carolina was named Wendell. He shared a bit about himself, and we exchanged phone numbers.

I usually don't call first, but the following day, he called me while I was at the beauty salon and wanted to hang out. He came to the salon, and we had a fun day running errands across the city—getting food, beauty supplies, and even some drinks. He seemed to enjoy helping out and appeared to be a hustler, but definitely not a broke one. Can you say rebound?

We spent my birthday weekend together since my kids were with their father. Because of a promise I made to my children, I told Wendell that he couldn't meet them and needed to leave before they came home. He became slightly upset and accused me of acting like a pimp. I calmly responded, "Relax, Wendell, all in good time. If you prove to me that you genuinely care about my well-being, you will meet my kids."

My lease was ending soon, and I was worried about finding a more affordable place to live. It was important for me to stay in the same area so my kids wouldn't have to change schools. I was also concerned about coming up with the money for moving deposits. Wendell showed up unannounced one day, insisting on meeting my children.

To be honest, he wasn't really my type. He was a bit radical, always talking about the Illuminati and secret societies. However, I decided it was time for me to get payback and give men a taste of their own medicine. I told Wendell I needed $2,000 to move, and he said he would have it for me in three days.

PAPER CHASE

Three days later, he returned to my house with groceries and $3,000. I guess he thought that would earn him something intimate. Not a chance! I made it clear that I wasn't interested in anything physical. I allowed him to hang out, but I told him to stay on his own side of the bed. I showed him some affection to keep him interested, but I had no desire to sleep with him. My children couldn't stand him because of his constant talk about conspiracies and other wild theories.

Ultimately, I realized my kids' feelings were worth much more than a few hundred dollars a week, so I decided to ask Wendell not to come around anymore.

We moved into a cute little house in the same area so the kids could attend the same schools. Before deciding to move, I had only visited the neighborhood during the day. However, once night fell, it transformed into what felt like the ghetto. People would set up their barbecue grills in their front yards and blast music from their cars. Since many of them didn't have jobs, they seemed to think

PAPER CHASE

it was acceptable to keep the noise until 2 a.m. There were constant fights, and the police lights were a common sight. Kids would be running up and down the street, screaming and hollering at 10 p.m. Out of twenty people on our block, twelve were receiving Section 8 assistance.

Two households stood out among the rest; they lived two houses apart from each other and both were named Robin. We'll call one "Chicago Robin" and the other "Lazy Robin." Chicago Robin, as the name suggests, was from Chicago and had a husband. They were taking full advantage of the system, paying only $200 a month in rent for one of the biggest and nicest houses on the block, while also receiving major government benefits, including substantial food stamps.

Chicago Robin was noisy yet surprisingly nice, and she kept it real. She took a liking to my girls and promised to look out for them because her next-door neighbor was a perv. Her husband also took a liking to my son, but there was something about him that made me uncomfortable. I usually struggle with men who give off that "wife-beater vibe." They had six kids with another on the way, plus at least ten dogs. Even though her kids ran wild and caused trouble, she made sure they were fed, clothed, and clean, which I couldn't say for Lazy Robin.

Lazy Robin was from Phoenix and had a house full of kids—at least fifteen of them. Most of her kids would run up and down the street barefoot, often wearing dirty clothes, if they wore clothes at all. To this day, I still couldn't tell which ones were hers. She was receiving government assistance and SSI, reportedly bringing in over $4,000 a month, not including food stamps. To say the least, she was not managing her situation like Chicago Robin. Lazy Robin hardly ever had food in her house and frequently borrowed everything from me, ranging from a cup of sugar to a sandwich. One evening, while I was cooking dinner, she sent one of her kids over to borrow sugar. When he smelled the food, he even asked if he could borrow a pork chop instead.

PAPER CHASE

Before long, "For Sale" signs went up in several yards; the other neighbors feared that it could only get worse, and they were correct. Meanwhile, my 15-year-old son was out of control—fighting, stealing, drinking, having sex, smoking weed, and committing crimes. I knew a man named Faraq who owned a construction company. Faraq had done some work on the restaurant I owned. My son seemed to light up when Faraq was around; he was nice, hip, and a believer. Raised as a Muslim, he had a near-death experience that led him to convert to Christianity. Faraq was handsome and knew it. He dressed well, and his style could have graced the cover of a fashion magazine. He often received compliments about looking like Denzel Washington.

I reached out to him and asked if he would mentor my son, and he gladly agreed. Faraq began coming over 3-4 times a week to pick up my son; sometimes they would stay at our house, while other times, they would go out. My son even worked part-time for him, earning decent money to help our household. Unfortunately, the marijuana had created a chemical imbalance in my son, making him act like a straight-up dope fiend. Within two months, he was expelled from school, taken to jail multiple times, and charged with a felony. Despite Faraq's efforts to help, my son chose his own path, which ultimately landed him in juvenile detention. I appreciated Faraq immensely for taking time out of his schedule to assist us. He even contributed to our groceries since he was over so often. I often found myself wishing he were younger.

As time went on, Faraq and I became very good friends. We talked about various topics, including politics, women's behaviors, and his long-distance relationship at the time. We prayed together and supported each other during difficult days. He was amazing—always willing to help with handy work without any obligation, and he was consistently present whenever my children and I needed assistance. I believe God sent him to us; he was always respectful and never made any advances towards me, which I truly appreciated.

PAPER CHASE

CHAPTER THIRTEEN

Keith and I were finally on cordial terms. I felt the need to forgive him in order to move on with my life. His health was deteriorating; he had respiratory issues, and diabetes was causing a multitude of complications. Despite this, I had no interest in reconciling with him. He still repulsed me and was no comparison to what James had put me through. I am forever changed, and no amount of Viagra could ever help Keith perform at that level.

Keith called to say he would need to have a pacemaker implanted to save his life. I gathered the children to explain the situation to them. I didn't even know what I would do if he didn't make it. The surgery lasted nine hours, and finally, the doctors emerged with good news. He would need a caretaker and assistance as he recovered. Since Keith lived alone at the time, I checked on him frequently, picked up his prescriptions, and brought him plates of food. He had little appetite and was losing a lot of weight.

PAPER CHASE

Faraq was proud of me for helping Keith. He was spending a lot of time with his ex-wife, who had recently suffered a stroke. Since Keith had not been able to work, he started receiving short-term disability benefits. I knew it was unlikely he would ever return to the workforce, so I suggested we file for SSI Disability. Keith had an older lady he was dating, and I hoped she would support him during this time. My girls mentioned that she was nice and thought she might be a nurse. Keith's grandmother humorously suggested I treat him like the character in one of Tyler Perry's movies, where the abused wife left him in the bathtub—she was quite the character.

Monica had a teenage daughter, and during one conversation, she mentioned how proud she was of me for taking care of so many girls when just one girl drove her nuts. We laughed, and she advised, "Cuz, you should really make sure all the girls are on Depo-Provera birth control; you don't need any more trouble." I told her I would look into it, and we said goodbye.

PAPER CHASE

Between my son and Keith, I was either late to work or had to leave early. My absences were beyond my control, so I kept my employer fully informed about the court proceedings and the trips to the emergency room with Keith. My son continued to get arrested and was on probation. I had to attend court so often with him that I felt like I was saying, "Your Honor," in my sleep. I was required to put him into a drug treatment program and arrange for both a psychiatric and psychological evaluation. He was stealing money from my purse and selling our household valuables without any remorse. I didn't believe in giving medication to kids, but in my opinion, he needed some sort of support.

I was at work, minding my own business, when my supervisor called me into her office. She explained that I was in violation of the attendance policy for leaving work early too often, and, as a result, I was being terminated. I couldn't believe this was happening. Did God now hate me? This had to stop; every time I turned around, there seemed to

PAPER CHASE

be another challenge to overcome. I was determined not to cry. While she was trying to explain her reasoning, I suddenly stood up from the small chair in the room and headed for the door. She followed me, along with another supervisor, walking briskly as if they were afraid I would damage their property. I had never been fired from a job before.

On the drive home, I immediately began to think of a plan to continue providing for my family. By the time I got home, I had it figured out. I would start selling food during the week at barbershops and beauty shops, and I would fill out legal documents for a fee for those who needed help. I decided not to tell anyone that I had been fired. The next morning, I woke up and headed to the law library at the courthouse. Having done my own divorce, I was fairly good at understanding legal documents. I offered to help a couple of people who appeared to be struggling with their forms and told them to call me later. When they did call, I would inform them of my fee and complete their paperwork.

PAPER CHASE

This became my job for 2-3 days a week. When I wasn't at the law library, I was at the barbershop selling ribs, catfish, chicken, and collard greens. I even made salads and sandwiches for those who were more health-conscious. I barely slept, thanks to Keith, who moved to Tucson with his girlfriend because I couldn't handle his needy behavior anymore, especially with everything else happening in my life.

I decided to make a business proposition to the Asian woman who rented to me. She owned several properties in the area, so I offered to maintain the landscaping by hiring someone. Most of the landscapers spoke Spanish, and since she barely spoke English, I convinced her to let me handle the hiring because I spoke Spanish (at least, that's what I told her). We ended up completing the landscaping ourselves—my children and I—and that extra money was just what we needed to buy essential items. I would tell my kids, "Act like you know; it's survival of the fittest, sink or swim."

PAPER CHASE

I had been working so hard and was getting really tired of the steady grind. But I kept pushing through because I had to pay the rent, and Keith still wasn't contributing. At that point, my two daughters, my son, Keith's daughters, and my Bonus Daughter all lived with me. I continued to confide in Farak about what had happened with my job and how we had been managing without it. He was amazed but also a little angry that I hadn't mentioned it sooner. He offered to pay a couple of bills to help us get through this rough patch, which was exactly what I needed; it would give me some time to pursue a real job. Thank you, Jesus, again. I had been doing a lot of soul-searching and asking God for direction. I was becoming weary and even lonely, which was odd considering all the kids in the house. I would rise at 3 AM each morning to work on my various money-making projects, and at the end of the day, I would be in bed by 8 PM to have the energy to work hard the next day.

PAPER CHASE

Then my son got arrested and was going to spend at least three months in juvenile detention for fighting and failing a drug test. Through prayer, I felt directed to enroll in college and apply for a position with a national retailer that had a call center in my area. Graduation was approaching; my second oldest daughter, referred to as "Lil Mamma," was graduating from high school as a junior and headed straight to a university with a full academic scholarship. My Bonus Daughter was also graduating and would attend community college in the fall. My eighth grader was set to graduate and would be moving on to high school. Their grandpa, Keith's father, decided to come down from Illinois, and I had so much to do to prepare the kids for their special day. I needed to pay for the hairdresser, new clothes, graduation gowns, and pictures. I had no idea how I was going to make all this happen while still paying the bills.

I started my online classes, but it was challenging for two reasons: I hadn't been to school in almost 20 years, and I wasn't getting enough rest.

PAPER CHASE

I hadn't been sleeping well because of nightmares. I typically didn't dream often, but when I did, it was usually about something bad on the horizon. I couldn't withstand any more negativity. I wanted to be a better person and stop cursing, smoking, and drinking altogether. Although my bad habits had faded significantly due to lack of time and energy, drinking at night would help me sleep despite the nightmares, but I always woke up as a nervous wreck the following morning.

I focused on graduation week. With the kids' grandpa in town, I called my beautician, and she agreed to close the shop to pamper me and my five girls. I handed her $600, and she styled our hair beautifully. The next day, I sent everyone shopping for new outfits, giving each of them $200 to get what they needed. My second-oldest daughter, "Lil Mamma," had started dating a boy from church earlier that summer. He drove her and my Bonus Daughter to the mall, while the other children rode with me. They all looked great and were thankful for the haircuts and shopping.

PAPER CHASE

I was so busy that I thought going out to eat after graduation would be the best option. Keith drove down from Tucson, trying to make a short visit. I told myself, I'll dare him to try to tell me what to wear or dictate where we should eat when he can't even contribute financially. I kept him on 'ignore' status the entire time, but remained civil for the children's sake.

The next morning, after a night filled with nightmares, I woke up and knew exactly who I needed to talk to. A small voice in my head urged me to speak with my 13-year-old daughter, who was going to turn 14 in just two days. The dreams I had were definitely about her. I went into the room she shared with my Bonus Daughter and began to ask her about her emotional state. I had noticed she had been unusually quiet and withdrawn, but I thought it was because Keith was around.

It struck me that she hadn't asked me to buy any feminine products for her. So, I asked her, "Have you had your period?" She lowered her head and shook it from side to side. I started feeling light-headed and gathered the courage to ask, "Are you pregnant?" She replied, still looking down, "I think so." I began to cry; the pain I felt was reminiscent of when my big momma died. My baby? Pregnant? How could I have let this happen? I quickly got dressed and ran to the drugstore to buy a pregnancy test, crying uncontrollably the whole way; I'm sure the staff thought the test was for me.

When I got back home, I asked her to come into the bathroom with me to take the test. Sure enough, it was positive—she was pregnant. I called Keith, desperate to understand how this could happen. I was always home; where could she have gone to have sex? She was only 13! I gathered all the kids together, and it turned out that while I was sleeping, a neighborhood boy and his sister had climbed through her bedroom window. Apparently, my Bonus Daughter is bisexual and had been fooling around with a girl, who brought along her 17-year-old brother for my 13-year-old daughter. What the hell!

PAPER CHASE

I became enraged. "What's the boy's phone number?" I demanded, and she reluctantly gave it to me. All the children were aware of what had been happening, but they chose not to snitch on each other.

The next morning, I felt like I was in a nightmare. I should have put her on birth control. I felt it was entirely my fault, regardless of the circumstances. I was extremely upset with my perverted Bonus Daughter and felt as if all the kids had let me down, throwing their baby sister to the wolves. Keith was devastated and immediately said she would have to get an abortion. He cursed me out, telling me what a horrible mother I was and that I was nothing more than a whore for being involved with Faraq. I guess he thought this was the perfect opportunity to meddle in my personal life. I gave him a piece of my mind. My only priority was to take care of the kids, and I wouldn't have to work so hard if he helped even a little. I told Keith that we would let my daughter decide what to do after she had all the facts about childbirth, the costs, and the responsibilities of having a baby. I called the boy involved, and he claimed he would take responsibility for the child and help my daughter.

Keith said he wasn't feeling well. We had had a very emotional day, and since he had a pacemaker, I didn't want to risk anything else bad happening. So, I took him to the emergency room to get checked out. When we arrived, they took us straight into a room because of his medical history, plus he was experiencing some chest pain. The hospital informed us that somehow his pacemaker had become disconnected and he would need surgery to repair it. Keith was admitted, and surgery was scheduled for the next day. His father had already returned to Illinois, so I called him to let him know Keith would have surgery on his pacemaker in the morning. I went home to shower and check on the kids, telling them about Keith and assuring them everything would be fine. After all, they were just reconnecting his pacemaker.

PAPER CHASE

On the morning of the surgery, I arrived at the hospital bright and early. I visited with Keith and spoke with the cardiologist before the procedure. After six hours, the receptionist yelled, "Family of Keith Lawrence!" I picked up the phone, and it was Dr. Lasco, the cardiologist, saying he would be right out. When the doctor came out, he was accompanied by his office assistant, Kathy. They began to explain that there was an issue during the surgery, and Keith suffered a massive stroke while they attempted to reconnect the pacemaker. The stroke completely took away his ability to speak and he could not feel the left side of his body. When they finally allowed me to see him, tears were streaming down his face, and he could not communicate. The prognosis was not good regarding his recovery and the likelihood of having another stroke. I called his father and told him to come back.

Meanwhile, I had to take my thirteen-year-old to the OBGYN; as we expected, she was pregnant. My daughter and I discussed the situation in detail,

PAPER CHASE

and she expressed her desire to have an abortion. I called the boy, who had fathered the child, to set up a meeting with him and his mother, as they would need to help cover the abortion costs. I was personally against abortion, but it was her choice; she wanted the opportunity to complete her education and be successful before having a child. The boy said his mother wasn't available and would call me back. After three days without a call, my oldest daughter and I went to his house. My Bonus Daughter had given us the address. We knocked on the door for at least ten minutes before anyone answered. They must have figured we weren't leaving. Uncle Ben, an old man, opened the door and said the boy's mother, Becky, was not home, of course. I told him I had personal business to discuss with her regarding my daughter and her son.

A few hours later, my phone rang; it was an unknown number. The lady on the other end claimed to be the boy's mother. I explained the whole situation and informed her that they would need to assist with the cost of the abortion. She agreed. My daughter was about two months pregnant, and the procedure would cost $600.

Later that day, Keith was released from the hospital after spending four weeks there and came to live with us. He shared a bedroom with my Bonus Daughter , but I no longer wanted her near her younger sister. Keith needed to learn how to speak and walk all over again. A speech therapist, a physical therapist, and a nurse visited him every day. My house literally smelled like a hospital. Meanwhile, I was still attending school online, cooking, filling out legal documents, and looking for a real job. Because of all the recent issues—pregnancy and the stroke—I wasn't making much money. I just didn't have the time or energy to keep grinding.

I scheduled the procedure for my daughter to have an abortion and called back to discuss their portion of the costs. The woman on the other end of the line had the nerve to tell me that her son was now claiming he wasn't the father and suggested I should tell my daughter to keep her legs closed. I

PAPER CHASE

was already on edge and this pushed me over. My oldest daughter overheard my argument with the boy's mother, and her anger grew with each moment. I calmly started getting dressed while we argued back and forth on the phone. I grabbed "Nina," my 9mm STS, and headed out the door.

When I arrived at her house, I calmly asked her to come outside. The line went quiet, and she hung up. After a few minutes with no movement from her house, I started banging on the door, trying to break it down. "Come outside!" I yelled. I stalked the house for at least an hour, but no one came in or out. Once I returned home, my phone rang again—an unknown number. That woman was still talking nonsense. I told her that I planned to prosecute her son for statutory rape since he was 18, and my daughter was only 13 when the conception occurred. That got her attention, and she abruptly hung up.

I went back to their house, and my oldest daughter jumped into the truck to come with me. I encountered Uncle Ben at the door again, and he

PAPER CHASE

informed me that the mother was out of town. I wasn't very nice this time. I told him I had just spoken with her and that they weren't going to keep playing games with me. I instructed him to call the police because they could talk to him about his stepson when they arrived. He refused, saying he would call Becky to ask what was going on. I left and cruised through the neighborhood in search of that boy. My daughter thought she saw him, so I pulled up on the curb where he was walking and jumped out of the truck. With the safety off, I confronted him and made it clear that he wouldn't see tomorrow. I heard my daughter scream, "It isn't him! It isn't him, Mom!" At that moment, the boy suddenly smelled terrible. I backed up slowly, got back in the truck, and drove away. I wasn't sure if the police were looking for me; I felt completely out of control. Ultimately, I just wanted to ensure my daughter was safe. It was about the principle of the matter—she and her son had to face the consequences.

PAPER CHASE

The day my daughter's procedure was scheduled was very warm, and I felt upset because my mother kept calling to tell me I was going to hell for taking a life. I felt like a zombie as we searched for the clinic's address. Suddenly, for no apparent reason, I turned into the wrong lane. A car was headed straight for us; it swerved to avoid a head-on collision and crashed into a large oak tree, which must have been 100 feet tall and 8 feet wide. Oh my god! I didn't know whether to turn around or keep going. I decided to turn around and get out of the car. Immediately, I asked the woman who had exited her vehicle if she was okay. She replied that she was fine, though her car was totaled, and the airbags had deployed. A man who witnessed the accident advised her not to speak to me. I shot him an "evil eye," as Big Momma used to say; I knew he would rather see me in a lot of trouble because of this incident.

I walked back to my car, and the man ran over to take a picture of my license plate. I planned to stay until the police arrived, and what that nosy man didn't realize was that I wasn't about to take any nonsense from him. One more word from him, and he was going to get an earful.

When the police arrived, the other driver was ticketed, and I was free to go. Just think of what could have happened if I had left the scene! We were now an hour late for our appointment. Was this a sign that we shouldn't go through with it? After the procedure, my daughter was very upset and crying. She said it was "really hard." I felt terrible that she had to go through that, and I still felt like I let her down—it was my fault. I should have protected her. All I could hear were Monica's warnings to protect my girls from premature pregnancy. My bad. I had just been so consumed with survival mode that nothing else mattered.

I needed a drink and some fresh air away from the house, so I called Monica. She always knew what was going on. We headed to a local "Hole in the Wall" to have a few drinks, listen to some music, and dance. I encountered people I hadn't seen in over a year. We played dominoes and a bit of spades on the patio. However, I couldn't get all my problems out of my mind. My heart felt like it was broken into a hundred pieces. I could only manage to drink one glass of cognac, which was unusual for me because I could usually hold my liquor. For some reason, that drink just didn't sit right, nor was I having as much fun as I normally would.

I turned to Monica and said, "Cuz, I'm ready to go. I don't feel good." She replied, "Okay, Cuz, drop me off at this other spot first," and we headed toward the car. "Damn, I feel dizzy and strange," I said. Monica responded, "Hold on; I'm going to get you some water." I walked back to the front of the club, drank the water she brought me, and waited until I felt better. Monica asked, "Damn, Cuz, how much did you drink?" I replied, "I didn't even finish one drink." "Weird," she said. We then headed back toward the car to leave, got in, and drove away.

PAPER CHASE

The other spot was probably five miles away, so I planned to drop Cuz off and go home. While I was driving, I started feeling dizzy again; something was wrong. Suddenly, my head became heavy, and I felt a piercing pain in the front of my head. I briefly blacked out and hit my head against the steering wheel. I immediately looked for a safe place to pull over. Still disoriented, I veered toward the turning lane, and just then, I saw red and blue lights. What the heck? Monica quickly began to explain the process; I had never even had a traffic ticket, let alone been to jail. She said, "You're about to get a DUI. They'll take you to jail, but we'll come get you tonight. Just don't answer any questions."

The officer approached and asked for my license and registration. After checking my documents, he asked me to step out of the car and questioned me about where I had been and where I was headed. I told him I was picking up my cousin. I knew I hadn't had enough to be considered drunk. He asked me to take a Breathalyzer, and it registered below the legal limit. So then, why was

PAPER CHASE

he still bothering me? He explained that because I had driven within one hour of drinking, even if I wasn't over the limit, it was still considered a DUI. In my state, if you are impaired to the slightest degree, it is considered a DUI.

My life was about to take a turn for the worse. Recent news highlighted that DUI laws in my state are among the strictest in the nation. The penalties were severe, including hefty fines and mandatory jail time. I was handcuffed, arrested, and taken to the police station, where I was photographed, fingerprinted, and given a blood test. After all that, I was released, and Monica was already outside waiting for me with one of her male friends. I felt humiliated. A DUI? Really? I had a court date in ten days, and I was anxious to find out what my punishment would be.

On the day of court, when the judge finally called me up, he had questions about a drug called Rohypnol found in my blood. I insisted that I didn't use drugs and had no idea how this could have happened. He directed me to speak with the prosecutor, who offered me a plea deal: a $3,000 fine, one day in jail, a series of defensive driving classes, and a requirement to install an ignition interlock device for one year.

Even though it seemed that I had been drugged without my knowledge, I still drove less than an hour after realizing I was impaired. I was completely baffled; my drink never left my sight, and I have no idea how this could have occurred.

PAPER CHASE

CHAPTER FOURTEEN

After about six months, Keith was feeling better, so I suggested he go down to Tucson to visit his lady friend—girlfriend, or whatever he called her. I just knew I needed a break. I would come home from working on my main money-making projects, and that guy would be in my bed. Oh, hell no! Not to mention, he would invade my space, trying to get a little too friendly. He repulsed me, and I was not about to have sex with him.

Keith was growing increasingly irritated by Faraq's frequent visits and calls to the house. My son was out of juvenile detention, so it was back to business for Faraq and my son; they seemed to enjoy each other's company. However, my son seemed to despise Keith. I appreciated Faraq, as he had battles of his own; his ex-wife had suffered another stroke and was now on life support in the hospital. Sadly, Faraq's ex-wife passed later that week, and of course, I went to the hospital to comfort their family.

PAPER CHASE

On the day of her funeral, it rained heavily. The cemetery where she was buried was 50 miles away from where we lived, and Faraq was having car trouble that week, so he borrowed my truck to drive to the funeral.

To my relief, Keith was visiting his girlfriend in Tucson every two weeks, and it was clear he was going to make a full recovery. I suggested he move in with her; I needed to get on with my life and make some changes. Moving out of this neighborhood and getting a fresh start for everyone was first on my list.

I finally received the call I had been waiting for; the local retailer wanted to schedule an interview for the position I had applied for months earlier. By early September, we were all settled into the new house. Everyone appreciated the new place—it was an older home that had been completely remodeled and was $500 less expensive than our previous home. The kids weren't crazy about the school, but as the mom, I said we needed a fresh start, all of us.

PAPER CHASE

I was offered a position working for the local retailer in a call center and would start in early October. Thank you, Jesus—things were looking up! I also accepted a part-time position working in the catering department at the Cardinals' stadium on game days. That same week, my dad's sister, Aunt Donna, called and told me to come by; she had a way for me to make some extra money as well. She always stayed in contact with me. Aunt Donna worked as a dispatcher and bred AKC-certified Boxers. Things were turning around just as quickly as they had gone bad.

The feud with Keith was reignited; he had the audacity to throw a lavish birthday party for himself while not contributing a single dime for the kids. I was furious because we were still struggling. With a full-time job, I didn't have much time to focus on my creative money-making projects. Keith had been denied SSI Disability benefits twice, so I hired a lawyer to help him appeal the decision. Although he had started receiving Long Term Disability benefits from his previous employer, he still claimed that he did what he could for the kids when we were apart. He insisted that whenever he had a little money, he spent some on them. He even said that he had been there to help me out during tough times, like when my truck was impounded and I would have had to walk otherwise.

Keith refused to accept any responsibility, claiming that he always tried to help when he could, even beyond matters concerning the kids. He insisted that he put us first. However, we were all struggling, and it was the same old story. His perspective was delusional. If he offered any assistance during our more agreeable periods, it was likely because he expected something in return. For me, it has always been about the kids. Yes, Keith gave me a couple of hundred dollars when we were on good terms, but that money went toward bills, not on luxuries like hair weaves or shopping trips.

PAPER CHASE

Keith was selfish, prioritizing his own needs while flaunting his lifestyle with his new girlfriend, going on trips and clubbing constantly. This selfishness had always been a pattern for him; he pursued whatever made him feel good without considering anyone else's feelings. If he couldn't get sex and attention in one place, he would simply seek it elsewhere. That was his version of happiness.

My oldest daughter was nearing the completion of her associate's degree when she landed a job and moved into her own place. My second-oldest daughter was living in the dorms at the university, so the only kids at home were my Bonus Daughter, my son, and my two younger daughters, who were then twelve and fourteen. My youngest daughter was quiet; she mostly just sat back and observed her older siblings. She was probably the only one who truly cared about Keith. Occasionally, Keith would send me a text message saying he loved me. He had to be nuts for saying that because he allowed the kids and me to suffer and didn't do anything to help us.

My Bonus Daughter was nineteen and showed no ambition whatsoever. She seemed to think it was acceptable to live off me, practically refusing to even look for a job. One morning, after working a sixteen-hour shift, I was getting ready for work when I accidentally dropped the ironing board. This girl yelled from another room, "Keep it down! I'm trying to sleep." Um, no! I had a talk with my Bonus Daughter later that day, explaining that she needed to think about her future and make her own way. I gave her five months to at least try to find a job. However, our talk seemed to mean nothing to her. Over the next few months, she continued her same routine: going to school, being promiscuous, coming home at 3 AM, and eating all the food in the house.

My second-oldest daughter (whom I called "Lil' Mamma") spent a lot of time at her boyfriend's house and often invited my Bonus Daughter over to hang out. I thought this was great because maybe she could influence her to pursue her goals. My

PAPER CHASE

college student was still a virgin and had decided she would hold out until marriage.

One day, while I was out catering, I stopped by Aunt Donna's house to check on the puppy. Aunt Donna was sitting in her well-manicured backyard that looked like a Caribbean retreat. She always seemed concerned about my financial situation and offered to help me with catering. I could have used her help that day, but I didn't want to bother her. I had heard from one of my other sisters that Aunt Donna was not feeling well. The puppy was ready to come home. Aunt Donna wanted me to have a girl so I could breed Boxers as well. She knew we loved dogs and would take good care of her. I decided to keep it a surprise for the kids and pretended I had left something in the car that I needed them to retrieve. When they saw the puppy, they screamed with joy and excitement, smiling from ear to ear and arguing over who would get to sleep with her. After much deliberation, we named the puppy Starr. My oldest daughter even came over to give the puppy

PAPER CHASE

her shots and check-up; it was great to have a veterinary tech in the family.

Finally, the day had come! May arrived, bringing my Bonus Daughter's deadline with it. She decided to pack up and leave without saying goodbye or even thanking me for my many years of parenting. She moved in with a woman from our church. She arranged to live with this lady without having to pay rent because her "job" was to take care of the woman's five children, each from different fathers. I was so disappointed in my Bonus Daughter because she had so much potential. The lady from the church better not let me catch her slipping. How could she tell someone's daughter that it's okay not to work? Just take care of my kids for me. What on earth was wrong with her? If I see her, I'll be ready to confront her.

"Three hundred dollars didn't just walk out of my purse," I told my son. "How could you do this? As hard as I work? Where is my motherfucking money?" He was high as a kite and wouldn't say a word. I called Faraq to tell him what happened, and he came right over. I was so hurt and frustrated with my son that I figured I'd better go for a ride because I wanted to smash him upside the head with Nina. While I was gone, Faraq arrived. The girls said they heard yelling and what sounded like a scuffle, and then Faraq stormed out. I wasn't concerned at all because I trusted him. I knew he loved all of us.

I called Faraq, but he didn't answer. Three days went by, and he still didn't call me back. I asked my son what happened that same night, but he wouldn't respond. I can't catch a break; I need Faraq. I love our conversations, and he is a great friend and confidant.

My son had returned to his old behavior. He was still on probation and had to be home by a certain time, which never happened. I called his probation officer to discuss the results of the urinalysis. I suspected he was using more than just weed this time; my daughters and I were kind of scared of him. He was talking to himself and pacing the floor all night. I had to sleep on top of my purse, and I suspected he had stolen my laptop and sold it because it just disappeared one day. The probation officer informed me that my son had failed the urinalysis again, but it was only for marijuana, which surprised me. His probation had been violated, and they planned to pick him up. Either my son didn't want to face me or he knew he had been violated, so he turned himself in at the juvenile detention center. We had court later that week, and the judge reprimanded him, possibly until the age of 18. He was only 16, and I didn't want him to go to Adobe Mountain, which was a high-level juvenile prison. Aunt Ladonna's son had gone there at 16, and to this day he is still in prison at 36. His life was ruined and he was not "rehabilitated" – he was institutionalized. As I thought about it, I realized the same thing had happened to Isaiah. This cycle was not going to control my son's life. I found myself wondering if something I didn't know about had happened to him that caused this behavior.

PAPER CHASE

After two weeks, Faraq finally called me. He said that as soon as he entered the room, my son attacked him. Faraq claimed my son thought he was only around to get close to me. Apparently, Faraq had shared with my son that he was in love with me, hoping to get his blessing. I was shocked because Faraq was always very respectful and never seemed to want anything more than friendship, despite all the time we spent together and the help he provided. He began to explain that he wanted my son's blessing because he didn't want to jeopardize their relationship and was concerned about my son's behavior. I let him know my son was now in juvie and could possibly be there until 18. Faraq immediately asked for the judge's information to write a letter and insisted on going to court with me for the next date.

Keith called me and said he was moving back to Phoenix because he wasn't getting along with his girlfriend. His oldest brother owned a townhome, which he would share with his brother Deven. Keith mentioned he would continue seeing his girlfriend but didn't want to live with her anymore. He also expressed the importance of repairing his relationship with his daughters. I was happy to hear he was thinking about his kids, but I couldn't shake the feeling that he would always have bad luck until he made things right with his son, who was conceived during our marriage.

Keith continued to face health issues and lacked healthcare benefits. I suspected his lifestyle contributed to his current health problems—he wasn't taking his medication and was drinking and smoking weed, which wasn't a good combination. I decided to add Keith to my health insurance as my significant other so he wouldn't suffer. I told him it would cost around $400 a month and asked if he could at least help me with $200 per month to offset the expense. Since Keith was still receiving Long Term Disability benefits, he agreed to contribute, and I was glad he was keeping his word.

PAPER CHASE

Despite multiple trips to the emergency room for Keith, things were going relatively well, and he was helping out with the agreed-upon $200. However, I started to feel overwhelmed. I was taking him shopping and doing his laundry on top of my other projects. My catering business had also increased in demand. Since he was still seeing his girlfriend, I suggested he ask her to take on some of the responsibilities. It felt crazy to be doing wifely things for a man I had no intention of being intimate with.

Amid all this chaos, I had been talking to a guy I met during graduation week, so I had known him for about a year. He was a breath of fresh air when we spoke on the phone. One day, he asked me when we would finally meet up in person. Although we had only communicated over the phone, after the year I'd had, I was hesitant about bringing anyone around my children. I wanted to set a good example for them and even told them that the next time I brought a guy home, it likely meant I was

PAPER CHASE

considering marriage. However, I had no plans of marrying Shameak.

Shameak was a handsome man born in New York, complete with an East Coast accent. He worked two jobs and took care of all his kids—yes, all seven of them, with the youngest being three years old. At 42 years old, he stood 6'2" tall and weighed 250 pounds of pure muscle—he had a six-pack. He even sent pictures to prove it. To be honest, one reason I hadn't hooked up with him was that I had never seen anything that large before, and I was a bit afraid. "No thanks!" was my thought on that!

During Labor Day weekend, my children were going to my niece's house to stay for a couple of days. I thought it would be the perfect opportunity to cook dinner for Shameak. He was always asking me about food and claimed he never got anything good. He had told me that as soon as he arrived, he expected a kiss that would make his body quiver.

PAPER CHASE

I prepared Monterey Chicken, Garlic Mashed Potatoes, Asparagus, Caesar Salad, and my signature buttermilk cake for dessert. He came over around 5 p.m. on Friday evening. Oh, my goodness— he was one of the finest men I had ever seen in my life; I couldn't compare him to anyone else. Naturally, I was looking and smelling good.

When I opened the door, he smiled as he stepped inside. I closed the door behind him and kissed him passionately for ten minutes. He exclaimed, "Whew, that was worth waiting a year for!"

We enjoyed dinner, laughed, talked, and drank some Cognac. In the back of my mind, I was still concerned that I couldn't handle him, but I had already decided I was ready to take that step with him.

Our conversation became intense; he told me that he needed to have me and couldn't wait any longer. I grabbed his hand and led him upstairs. He started undressing himself as we entered my bedroom and I followed his lead, undressing myself. He didn't seem to be that interested in foreplay but we kissed and he caressed my breasts as he attempted to enter my body. It would not fit; he whispered in my ear, "relax baby". He started to kiss and caress my entire body while he spoke softly to me. His words caused my juices to erupt like never before. Before I could catch my breath, he was inside my body moving slowly. I could hardly handle the pain of pleasure. I whispered to him that I couldn't take it, he again told me to relax. He had mind control and after three hours he still had not come. I begged him to stop because he was too large for me; I would have to get used to this. We spent the entire weekend together and watched movies during the rest of the time. I was concerned that I didn't satisfy him; but when he left on Sunday, he recorded a video and sent it to my phone. He said that the sex was "the bomb" and he couldn't wait to see me again.

Faraq and I were hardly speaking, and there were no new developments in my son's case. I was

PAPER CHASE

busy with my online classes, leaving little time for anything outside of studying. At least once a month, Tiffany, Agelique, and I would make time for ourselves. We'd catch a comedy show or head to a club in Scottsdale—whatever worked at the time.

Keith was getting increasingly frustrated because I didn't want to spend time with him and had stopped helping him out. I confided in Shameak about our situation, including the fact that I had added Keith to my health benefits. While Shameak never pressured me to meet my children, he often asked about them. To my surprise, he started contributing around $600 toward the bills without me asking him for anything.

Shameak would come over every night after the kids were asleep. I found that I needed to have a drink before our encounters, as I was still not fully comfortable with his generosity. Our time together was enjoyable, mainly due to the physical attraction I felt for him—just looking at him could arouse me.

PAPER CHASE

I continued seeing Shameak for nine months, but eventually, I grew tired of sneaking around behind my kids' backs. Deep down, I knew he wasn't husband material; he had too many children and too much baby mama drama for me—definitely No Bueno.

I called Shameak to let him know that I wanted God to bless me with a husband, and I felt that I couldn't pursue that while involved with him. He was furious and hung up on me. Before hanging up, he told me to never call him again. I suggested that we could remain friends, but he insisted that we could never be just friends in his eyes.

PAPER CHASE

CHAPTER FIFTEEN

Who is calling me at three in the morning? I picked up the phone, and it was my oldest daughter saying that my stepdaughter had called the police on her. What was going on now? My daughter explained that when my stepdaughter hung out with my second-to-oldest (whom we call "Lil Mama") and her boyfriend, some bad things were happening. Apparently, my stepdaughter was having sex with my daughter's boyfriends and calling my daughter to flaunt it in her face. Who does that kind of thing to my child? My oldest daughter was determined to confront my stepdaughter for this outrageous behavior. Meanwhile, my daughter's heart was broken.

I spoke to Lil Mama about the incident. She was devastated but planned on forgiving her boyfriend and even marrying him. I told her that if she could forgive him, she should also forgive her sister, considering that she didn't engage in those actions alone.

PAPER CHASE

I was so fed up with Phoenix that I needed to leave. I gathered the two youngest kids and told them I planned to start looking for a job in Memphis. Not only could I earn more money there while pursuing a degree, but we would also be closer to their grandpa (Keith's dad). The kids were excited; they must have been tired of all the drama too. I found a couple of positions, and my current supervisor said he could help me secure one within six months.

I visited my mom and told her we would be moving to Memphis no later than the beginning of next year. She was extremely upset and didn't want us to leave. I believed that moving to Memphis would provide an opportunity for better financial stability and possibly lead me to a good husband. It felt like I had gone through so much alone. I believed that every challenge I faced could ultimately benefit someone else. Long ago, my Big Momma had told me that my life would serve as an example for women and children who needed moral support. However, I wrestled with the fact that

PAPER CHASE

everything seemed to revolve around money for me. Yes, my ultimate goal was to provide for my family, but my focus felt misguided.

With the exception of delivering dinners for Big Momma when I was eight, every relationship or situation in my quest for money led to heartache. The experiences with Baby He, Tony, Ronald Black, my failed restaurant, and my various money-making projects were all painful reminders of my pursuit.

I continued to excel in my position at work, missing no days due to illness, drama, or any other reason. I always gave 150% in everything I did, and management took notice. As a result, I was given extra responsibilities and additional projects. I was even asked for my opinion on an important company issue. One day, my manager requested that I come into the boardroom for a meeting. I thought, "Oh no, I'm going to be on the news if anything bad is about to happen."

PAPER CHASE

My supervisor had my full attention when he told me I was a valuable employee and that there was talk of offering me a position on an elite negotiation team that was two pay grades higher, provided I would consider staying in town. I was overjoyed and told him I would stay because the opportunity to make money was the reason I was planning to leave in the first place.

I thought, perhaps this terrible 15-year nightmare was finally coming to an end. Thank you, Jesus. I'm not particularly religious, but I knew God heard my prayers; I had been crying out for help and direction, and He was probably tired of my pleas. I didn't tell anyone about the opportunity until I officially received the job offer the following Monday—Promotion Day! I was ecstatic and felt like I had finally accomplished something. I couldn't wait to share the news with my kids.

When I got home, I asked them to come into the living room to hear the great news. However, they seemed unemotional and just stared at me. My 15-year-old yelled, "So we're not moving to

PAPER CHASE

Memphis?" I replied, "No, we don't have to; this is great news! Aren't you happy?" She threw the biggest temper tantrum she had ever thrown because she didn't want to stay in Phoenix, which really dampened my excitement. I eventually had to threaten to discipline her to get her to calm down.

On the first day of my new position, I felt like I was walking on clouds. I was slightly in shock because I hardly had any work to do. I thought, "They're paying me all this extra money to just sit in this office." The best part was that the job was less stressful, better-paying, and had improved hours. I continued taking my online classes to pursue a degree in Business Communications.

During this time, I briefly spoke with Keith, who was heading back to Illinois for a funeral. One of his uncles had passed away from prostate cancer. My heart ached for the entire family; losing someone is difficult, especially for a tight-knit family. I had also experienced a loss that week—my Aunt Donna passed away from breast cancer. I hate cancer! When I was younger, diabetes seemed like the worst epidemic; now it's cancer, and it shows no mercy. This year alone, I have known or been acquainted with at least 12 people who lost their battle with cancer.

During our phone call, we reminisced about old times when we lived together in Illinois and the moments we spent with the uncle who had passed away. We said our goodbyes, and I asked him to extend my condolences to the rest of the family.

There was a little evil voice in the back of my mind reminding me that not only was Keith back working for his brother under the table, but it was also almost time for the hearing regarding the SSI disability benefits I had helped him apply for nearly two years ago. I knew that Keith always wanted to reconcile with me for some reason, and I wasn't sure why I had this hold over him. He would often tell me that no matter who he was with, he would drop them like a hot potato for the chance to be with me again. I had to come up with a plan because there was no way I would let some other woman get the money that was meant for his kids.

PAPER CHASE

Something sinister was definitely brewing in my mind. I thought about everything that Keith had put me and my family through, and I was determined to get payback. On a scale of one to ten, my anger and resentment towards Keith was at a hundred.

I had no physical attraction to Keith; in fact, he repulsed me. I'm not superficial and can usually look past physical appearance, but a person at least needs to be decent. In my opinion, Keith was the lowest of the low in the category of good human beings. He had mistreated both me and his kids, and the bad times far outweighed the good times where he was concerned.

When Keith returned from Illinois, he called and asked me to meet him somewhere to talk, and I agreed. I met him for dinner on a work night, and he reminded me that he only wanted to be with me. I made light of that, and we laughed and joked about random things. All the while, my motives for even spending time with him had never been darker. He looked at me intensely, and I could tell he was waiting for an answer from me about reconciling. I responded, "We can try it, but the old Stacy is dead. I buried her and spat on the grave. Can you handle that, Keith?" He responded that he was no longer the same either. He claimed to have realized the error of his ways and acknowledged how he mistreated me and the kids; he insisted he was no longer the judgmental and angry person he once was. In my mind, I heard the teacher from Charlie Brown, "Whomp, whomp, whomp." I'm no fool! I knew he would never change. Honestly, I couldn't care less because he wasn't going to have the chance to mistreat me again.

After dinner, Keith asked me to come home with him to make love. Are you serious? I had to compose myself; this man wanted me to go into another woman's house, into her bed, and have sex with him. Who did he think I was? I calmly replied, "I would never be caught dead in another woman's home." That night, I lost even more respect for him.

PAPER CHASE

How did I become so cold? I truly didn't care how any man felt at this point. If the situation wasn't going to benefit the children, it simply didn't matter to me. I could love them and leave them in the blink of an eye and feel nothing. I didn't even care about sex. I could take it or leave it.

Keith continued to call me each night, mostly to chat about his apologies for his past mistakes. One night, he mentioned he was having trouble getting along with his lady friend. At that point, I didn't know what to call her. He whispered on the phone, "I got a little trouble over here; I think I need you to come get me." What now? I hadn't even formulated my plan yet. Despite my dark feelings, I still had a soft spot for him. After all, it sounded like he was in trouble, so I headed over to get him. I had work the next morning, so as soon as we got back to my house, I went straight to bed. I didn't think twice about him staying over—for just one night—because after all, he was the father of my children.

My phone rang at 5 AM, and it was my sister, Stephanie. I answered, "Hey, sis," still half asleep.

PAPER CHASE

In an angry tone, she said, "My niece called me and said you have her dad in the room with you 'doing it'! How could you go back to your vomit? Seems like slaves always want to go back to Egypt." Stephanie had developed a strong dislike for Keith ever since that incident at the club when we were out with Monica. My plan wasn't going as expected; it wasn't supposed to go down like this. I didn't want anyone except the people who lived in my house to know that I was involved with Keith. I was so embarrassed that my 15-year-old had shared my business that you could have bought me for a dollar. I got up to ask my daughter about the phone call she made to my sister, but she gave me the silent treatment.

Later that day, while I was working, I received a text from my sister that read, "My niece no longer wants to live in your house, so we got her things, and I'll need her birth certificate to enroll her in school." At this point, I felt like my sister was completely out of line and probably needed some medication to get her thoughts together. I tried to

PAPER CHASE

calm down and see things from my daughter's perspective: 1. She disliked her dad for his treatment of us, and 2. She simply did not want him around.

I called my daughter and told her I didn't agree with the arrangement and that I would give her a couple of days to cool off before she needed to come home. She replied, "No, I'm not living in that house anymore!" I thought to myself, "Wooosah, I'll fight a kid! Who does she think she's dealing with?" I hung up to avoid becoming too angry and decided to let things rest for a day or two. My daughter might have thought I was planning to remarry him since I had promised not to bring anyone home if that were my intention.

I decided to step back and focus on finding a new home, so I contacted a local realtor. I didn't want to rent from a private owner again because the woman who owned my house never fixed anything. With Faraq not coming around to address repairs, the house might as well have been held up by a kickstand. I wanted a nicer home closer to my

PAPER CHASE

job so I could enjoy decorating it and save money on gas. I really disliked moving because it seemed like something valuable always broke in the process. I took good care of my belongings—furniture, knick-knacks, etc.—and worked hard for what I had.

After about three weeks, I found the perfect house for us. It had plenty of space, was all on one level, and was new. Now came the difficult part: I needed the money for the first month's rent, last month's rent, and the deposit—not to mention the utility deposits and moving truck costs. I had a large catering event scheduled that would provide me with a payment, so I felt it would all work out.

Keith was still sleeping over, and I didn't ask him any questions about what happened with his lady. Frankly, I didn't care. My main reason for dealing with him was to get his financial help, which he should provide. I called my sister and asked her to bring my daughter home. They had been running wild for over a week now, and my sister was in the wrong. She had been texting me all week, calling me stupid and saying she would never speak to me

PAPER CHASE

again. I reminded her that I didn't say anything about her husband not having a job for the first ten years of their marriage, and they had only been married for twelve years. We all have issues and probably deal with people we shouldn't, but she had no right to interfere like that. I also had a plan for Keith that she would never have imagined.

I told my sister we could resolve this in one of two ways:

1. I could come to get my daughter and call the police on her for picking her up from school without my permission, or

2. She could bring her home, and we could squash the whole thing.

I was frustrated, but I would never actually call the police on her. I realized she loved me and didn't want to see me back with Keith.

My client, who had a large event scheduled, called and requested a meeting, so I had to leave early for work. I informed Keith, as I had been dropping him off at his brother's office each morning on my way in. I wasn't sure how to implement my plan to just be "co-parents." I started hinting that he should work things out with his lady because I knew I didn't have romantic feelings for him.

After dropping Keith off, I headed to the coffee shop near my job to meet with my client. She wanted to meet face-to-face because her engagement was called off, and she needed to cancel her event. The reception was scheduled six months away, and according to the contract guidelines, she would receive a partial refund. This meant I not only had to refund her some money, but I also wouldn't get the funds I had expected to help finance my move. What would I do now?

Challenges never seemed to stop me; they only slowed me down. I always said that God really had my back and loved me despite my shortcomings. I ran the numbers—still not enough. I ran them again—still not enough. "SHIT!" I yelled. Keith was working and expected one last check from long-term disability. I ran the numbers again, and with the money Keith would provide, it would just be enough to get everything done. The last thing I wanted was to feel like I owed him anything; after all, he owed us. But accepting money from him felt like getting in bed with the devil.

I did it again: Keith was moving in with us, and I wasn't telling anyone. I was embarrassed about repeating history, but my mindset was completely different this time. I knew I wanted no part of the love he had to offer. Keith wasn't capable of being the mate, husband, or friend I needed. I viewed him as judgmental and toxic, and I had little respect for him because of how he had treated his children. After being involved with men like James and Shameak, I was used to a different type of guy in terms of appearance and ability. But I had little choice—I had already given notice to the owner of my current house, and it had been rented out, so I had to move into the new place as planned. God help us; this seemed like a recipe for disaster.

Keith was so proud of himself for contributing his meager amount; who was I to judge? I needed his money. Honestly, he was acting as if he was in charge of my life, like he was "Boss Hog." He had that "Yeah" feeling, as I called it, whenever he did something responsible. He was supposed to help, but he struggled with the whole "Yeah" feeling. My survival instinct kicked in, and I knew I had to let him know that I was the one in charge here.

When moving day arrived, everything was packed and ready to go. I had hired a moving company that someone had recommended to me. I followed up with them multiple times to ensure I was on the schedule and to go over the details of what type of furniture I had and how much other stuff I needed to move. My furniture included a very large king-size bed with pillars, a huge dresser, and oversized nightstands that required special attention.

The movers called to inform me that they were running late and would arrive in an hour. I thought, great! This is not a good start to the day because I had everything planned down to the minute, and I wanted to be done by a certain time to watch the Floyd Mayweather fight. I didn't know

PAPER CHASE

who he was fighting, but he was one of those fighters who always stole the show. If Floyd was involved, he was usually the only name anyone remembered.

I looked out the window and saw the movers pulling up with a trailer. Although it was fine, it seemed too small to move a three-bedroom house with all my belongings. I ran outside and asked, "Where's the real truck?" To make matters worse, there were only two guys, and I had explicitly requested three. "Where's the third guy?" I asked. One of the movers replied, "Aye." I repeated, "You don't speak English?" He responded with "Pequito," so I shot back, "Uno momento por favor, motherfucker." I grabbed my phone and called the owner of the moving company, who spoke perfect English.

"Hello, Stacey," he answered. I immediately expressed my frustration. "I'm distraught with this arrangement. They're late, one guy is missing, the trailer is too small, and they don't speak English." The owner assured me that the third guy was on the

PAPER CHASE

way and that he spoke English. He also claimed that all my items would fit because they were "professionals" who knew how to pack the trailer. I reluctantly accepted that and figured they might know what they were doing. I told him, "This process needs to go smoothly; all my things must go, and nothing can be left behind."

After hanging up, he called one of the movers who was already there. They had about a five-minute conversation in Spanish before the two guys got started. Three hours later, there was still no sign of the third guy, and I was paying $70 per hour. I told my children and Keith that we needed to help the movers get some of the stuff onto the trailer since I had only budgeted for ten hours.

The kids and I started helping out, while Keith sat in a chair in the garage to watch. Unbelievable! He didn't even have the decency to try to help. Sure, I know he can't lift heavy things, but at least he could have attempted to do something. Still, there was no third guy, and just as I feared, all my belongings did not fit in the trailer. I

PAPER CHASE

called the owner again, but he didn't answer. I called him from Keith's phone, and he answered on the first ring, "24/7 Movers, how can I help?" I started explaining my situation, but then I looked up and saw Pablo and Pablo Jr. wedging my $4,000 bed between the stairs. I screamed, "What the hell are you doing? It has to come apart!"

I told the owner what his "professionals" were doing, and he asked me to put one of them on the phone. They spoke in Spanish for just a moment, and then he handed the phone back to me. I managed to get them to understand that the bed had to be taken apart, but the mover grabbed a flat-head screwdriver and began stripping my screws. I screamed, "STOP!" Realizing they didn't have the appropriate tools, I grabbed my purse and headed to the hardware store. While driving, I tried calling the owner again, but he didn't answer. I was furious to the point of shaking. I could have hired some day laborers from in front of Home Depot and rented a U-Haul truck for a better experience.

PAPER CHASE

I arrived back at the house with the necessary tools to take apart my bed and noticed a car I didn't recognize parked outside. It must be the third guy, I thought. When I walked in, a big, burly Hispanic man introduced himself as the owner of the moving company. His two "professionals" were still struggling on the stairs with my bed wedged between them. I handed the owner the tools and asked him to consult his employees to ensure there were no further misunderstandings.

The owner spoke with me for a bit before leaving, and we agreed that I would pay $40 per hour instead of $70. Unfortunately, the third guy never showed up, but the owner assured me that all my things would fit on the trailer. The house was finally empty, and my bed and other nice pieces of furniture were safely loaded onto the trailer. However, the garage was still full of items, including boxes, Christmas decorations, catering equipment, televisions, and much more.

PAPER CHASE

I called the owner again to figure out the best way to move my remaining belongings to my new place. He told me they would make a second trip, but I would have to pay an additional gas surcharge. I refused to pay them another cent and was so frustrated with the useless self-proclaimed businessperson that I didn't know what to do. I told him, "What I'm going to do is never use your company or recommend it to anyone I know." Then I hung up the phone. What a fiasco! Now I had to figure out how to get the rest of my things to my new place, which was 50 miles away.

Once we arrived at the new place, everything was going smoothly until I opened the garage. I instructed the movers to place all boxes in the garage so we could unpack from there. As I opened the garage door, it suddenly crashed to the ground, completely coming off its hinges. Needless to say, my belongings and the house would be vulnerable. Anyone could have walked in and taken what they wanted. Son of a biscuit-eating bulldog! The realtor must have known the garage was broken. I had to

PAPER CHASE

laugh to avoid crying. What a day—one thing after another!

They finished unloading the truck, and after putting some sheets on my bed, I took a shower and went to sleep.

The next morning, Keith called his brother, Devin, who had access to his work truck and could help us retrieve the rest of our things. I met Devin at the old place, and we loaded the remaining items onto his truck. I was a little concerned that some things might fly off during the drive, so we reorganized some items until they were secure, and we headed out. We were finally finished!

Once we got back to the new place, I felt really good about having completed the move and immediately started unpacking. The first item I looked for was a suitcase full of old photos of my Big Momma and Grandma Henrietta. To my dismay, it was gone, along with several other things. I searched high and low but couldn't find the pictures. Apparently, while Devin was driving, a few

PAPER CHASE

items had fallen off his truck along the freeway, and he didn't feel the need to stop and retrieve them. I will never be able to replace those photos; in fact, I was the only one in the family who had a picture of Grandma Henrietta. I felt incredibly emotional about losing all those memories, and every part of me wanted to cry like a baby. I even had to stop myself from calling Devin and sharing some less-than-friendly words with him. I'm sure if he had known what was in that suitcase, he would have tried to retrieve it. Oh well, that's another loss I'll have to chalk up along with the others.

I haven't told anyone except Latrice that Keith is here, and since Devin helped us move the rest of my things, I was sure he would inform Monica. Monica has been there for me and the kids time and time again, and I knew she would be upset with me because she wouldn't understand why I was even associating with him, let alone getting back together. When we first met years ago, she recognized that I was being mistreated, and she didn't like it.

PAPER CHASE

Just as I expected, a couple of days later, Monica sent me a message saying, "Oh, y'all are acting brand new because you're back together." I took a deep breath, bracing myself for what I thought would be a harsh conversation, and dialed her number. When Monica answered, she said, "What's up, Cuz? Huh?" I thought, here we go.

She explained that she already understood my reasons for allowing Keith back into my life. Then, she went on to say that the whole situation baffled the rest of Keith's family. She concluded with, "Forget them! Do what you have to do, Cuz. I love you more, huh?"

PAPER CHASE

CHAPTER SIXTEEN

I completely understand that a man wants to feel valued and in charge, being the breadwinner of the family. Keith has been acting increasingly delusional lately, thinking he's in control of everything. I realized I needed to have a serious talk with him. I remembered our conversation over dinner after he returned from his uncle's funeral in Illinois. He had been getting out of control, yelling at the dog and talking crazy to the kids. We had always maintained a laid-back atmosphere with no arguing, as we knew that handling drama was best through calm conversations.

I asked Keith to take a ride with me, and we drove to a nearby park. I started the conversation by saying, "I really want this to work." Honestly, I wasn't even sure I wanted to be in this situation, but I continued. I explained that our arrangement was new, and we needed to do things differently without backtracking.

PAPER CHASE

I laid down some ground rules:

1. I discipline the kids.

2. Don't yell at the dog.

3. Absolutely no arguing in the house.

I also told him, "Remember, I said the old Stacey is dead. I buried her and spat on the grave." Keith looked frightened and replied, "Please take me home," in a weak voice. I drove him back, and he didn't speak to me for three days.

Then I found out he had punched and kicked our dog, Starr. "Nooooo!" I yelled at the top of my voice. "What the hell is wrong with you, Keith? Where do they do that?" Thankfully, the kids were staying at Stephanie's for the night. "You don't punch and kick your kid, so you certainly don't punch and kick your dog."

Keith yelled back, "She bit me!" Apparently, when I walked back into my room, Starr had jumped up on the patio door. Even though we had always told her "Down, Starr," she was just a puppy and not as obedient as we wanted her to be. Instead of telling her to get down, Keith tried to hit her but missed, causing himself to fall and scrape his elbow. In the process, Starr bit the same hand he tried to hit her with.

When I walked in and saw him chasing her into a corner and punching and kicking her, I confronted him angrily. "Don't you ever touch her again!" I warned. He followed me back to the kitchen, shouting, "You're choosing a dog over me?" I calmly started boiling a pot of water while we argued. Keith threatened, "You're gonna come home and not have a dog!" I replied, "You're being evil, Keith. There will be repercussions if you ever touch her again."

I was furious. "You're ten times her size! How could you corner her and hurt her that way?" We continued to argue as I poured a little vegetable oil into the boiling water. I told him, "I won't say it again: that is our dog, and we love her. We don't abuse her. Dogs jump on things; that's what they do."

PAPER CHASE

Before I could finish my sentence, Keith charged toward me. Deep down, I wanted him to get angry enough to confront me because I was ready to show him seriousness. I put on my oven mitt as he approached. He stopped in his tracks, looking me dead in the eye. If he had been a dog, he would have had his tail between his legs. I think he realized things were about to get ugly because, suddenly, he turned and quietly sat down on the couch.

I was still angry, cursing and yelling for about thirty minutes without receiving a response from him. Later, when the kids came home, I talked to them about how he treated Starr while I was at work. Apparently, this wasn't the first time he had hit the dog, and I was furious. They should have told me when it happened! My daughters said they didn't know what to do because they felt he would fuss at them when I wasn't home if they spoke up.

Sleeping in the same bed was going to be a problem. "I am not interested in sex with you," I told Keith. He replied, "A man can't feel like a man if he can't even have sex with his wife." Wife? Oh boy, I knew this was wrong. I was aware that he was attracted to me and believed he was in love with me. I wasn't sure how I was going to handle this situation. I decided to focus on the upcoming disability hearing, which could result in two years' worth of back pay. "Focus, Stacey," I told myself. I needed a plan to keep him off my back about sex. I came up with an excuse: "I have female problems." But how long would that excuse work? Help me, God. The thought of lying with this man repulsed me. On the other hand, it would only take two minutes, but even the idea made me feel sick. How did I endure it all those years?

Not only was I not interested in sex with Keith, but I also had no urge to be intimate with anyone. My mind was consumed with work, school, and restructuring my catering business. With my focus on earning a business degree and making money, I believed my success would inspire my children to pursue their own dreams. The two youngest girls were the only ones still living at home, while my son was expected to visit soon from

PAPER CHASE

military school. The girls actually enjoyed their schools, liked the area, and had made new friends. Life was starting to feel better than it had in a long time.

PAPER CHASE

CHAPTER SEVENTEEN

The new place is great. I had everything organized, and the décor looked fantastic. Unfortunately, the garage was still broken, and there were some other maintenance issues that the realtor was dragging her feet on. The realtor was really nice until she received my check, and then she seemed to change her demeanor. I started documenting all the necessary repairs in writing and provided her with a timeline to complete them; otherwise, I threatened to have the work done and deduct the cost from the rent. Mentioning the rent deduction definitely got her attention, and she began ensuring that things were fixed properly. However, one issue remained beyond her control: Arizona scorpions.

In all honesty, to quote Mary J. Blige, "All I really want is to be happy." My life had been a series of challenges, and even when things went

PAPER CHASE

well, I always waited for the other shoe to drop. Sadly, whether Keith was sincere or not, the damage was done, and it was too late. My heart felt locked away in a box and buried in the desert. I developed a habit of standing in front of the mirror each morning and saying, "I love you, Stacey." I finally learned to love myself more than anyone else, which is how it should be. Celebrate good times... come on!

While some issues were resolved, this was not how I envisioned my life. I wanted to feel complete and be in love. Throughout my life, the love of others had motivated my success, whether it was a love for money or a love for another person. I love my children, and I continued to work hard so they would always have what they needed. Still, my deepest desire was to have a complete, non-dysfunctional home life, husband included. I deserved that. I realized too much had happened between me and Keith, which prevented me from letting my guard down with him. I explained to Keith that I was still affected by how we were treated when we weren't together. If you love someone, why does it turn into an all-out feud when you're not with them? That's crazy.

I have moved past the physical and verbal abuse, and even the fact that there was a child outside of our marriage. Keith treated the kids like they didn't exist during our time apart, which is hard to digest. For instance, when he and I weren't on good terms, he refused to help at all. For me, it has never been about the amount of money because we always managed to get through tough times. However, Keith was still dealing with issues of his own. He once told me, "You'll do anything for a dollar." He also still had pictures of the woman he had been involved with on his camera. During a family function at his oldest brother's house, I was just trying to look at pictures we had taken when I stumbled upon pictures of Keith with her! They were together during a time when the children and I were struggling.

PAPER CHASE

That wasn't even my biggest issue with him keeping those pictures. I used to ask Keith, "Why would you want to identify with that part of your life if your family is the most important thing?" It just mirrored the cycle we had always been through. This wasn't the first time we had argued about pictures, internet dating, or inappropriate websites. Not to mention, the cable bill was still in his name at that woman's house.

I explained to Keith that when I initially let him come back, it was because I missed him and was tired of being alone. I missed family gatherings and felt left out. I wanted to feel special, go on movie dates, and receive gifts for no reason. Even though I knew I had started interacting with him out of necessity, I have to be honest about my feelings. I had reached a point where I didn't want to introduce anyone else to my daughters and wanted to set a better example for them. I thought their dad deserved a chance because I didn't want to worry about bringing some weirdo or creep around my girls. So, I figured I would try again with Keith.

PAPER CHASE

Eventually, I fell in love with the idea that he could change for the better. I knew he had a strong personality but wasn't a physical threat anymore due to his health issues. I believed that as long as he wasn't judgmental and didn't talk down to us, we could manage. However, shortly after he moved in, the old Keith returned, along with the resentment I felt toward him. I told Keith that I believed he had reverted to his old character, which I could no longer tolerate. I reminded him that he had claimed to understand me and said he had learned from our past mistakes. He promised he would make things right and improve our financial situation, even though I felt I had changed as a person, and not necessarily for the better.

Honestly, I felt like Erykah Badu was singing about me in her song "Bag Lady" — let it go, let it go, let it go.

"I'm not leaving," he said. "This is my house too!" An argument ensued, and I became filled with rage. "You haven't done even a quarter of what I've done to get this house! The lease has my name on it, so don't tell me what you're going to do!" I shouted.

"Whether it's a good or bad thing doesn't matter. If we're parting ways, I won't be the one to leave for obvious reasons." I calmed down and lowered my voice, remembering the kids were present. "Bottom line, Keith," I said softly, "this relationship is not working. We need to sort this out civilly because that's what's best for the kids." I told him that when he received his disability money, it would likely be enough to help him get back on his feet.

"If you can coexist peacefully in this house until things get sorted, I'm fine with that," I added. Keith responded, "Well, I'm going to do what makes me happy, and that will be without you if you don't jump on board."

In the nicest way possible, I told him, "Go ahead and do what you need to do to be happy now. I cannot be who you want me to be. I'm not happy with how things have turned out, but I think it's time

PAPER CHASE

we face the facts: it will never be like it was. I believe you have good intentions, but this is still not working."

Keith always seemed to need to be with a woman and, in my opinion, had an unhealthy appetite for sex. If I had let him, he would have wanted to be intimate with me even when I was on my cycle. Given his interpretation of "happy," what I really wanted to say was that the loving feeling is gone, and the thought of being intimate with him is repulsive!

I took the time to self-evaluate, both as a mother and as a person. Did I truly understand what made me happy and fulfilled? Over the years, I often chose money or the love of a man over my children. I can't erase my years with Keith, but looking back, I realize that I didn't love myself—I didn't love Stacey. How could I truly love someone else when I didn't love myself? Because of this flaw, my children suffered. It could have been worse, and thankfully no one I refer to as a monster ever violated my kids. I kept them safe from molestation, but they witnessed me battered and bruised, just as I had witnessed my mom endure the same, and she had seen her mother experience it too, just as my Big Momma witnessed her mother (Grandma Henrietta) going through it.

My children saw me cry and stressed out, to the point where I was unable to focus on their emotional needs, and for that, I have asked them to forgive me. While we all choose our own paths and should understand the difference between right and wrong, I must take full responsibility for who my children are and who they are not. My stepson is in prison; my stepdaughter struggles with loyalty, honesty, and self-worth, and she currently calls a stranger "Mom." My oldest daughter is managing well after facing numerous challenges. My youngest daughter is allowing a man to mistreat her and has low self-esteem. My son is in a boys' home as an alternative to prison, and my 15-year-old was pregnant at just 13. Ironically, my youngest seems to possess the most wisdom, but she remains mysterious.

PAPER CHASE

No matter where my children are in life right now, I realize I played a part in their journeys. I know everyone chooses their own path, but they relied on me for guidance, and I feel like I let them down. Regardless of their circumstances, I will always be there for all of them through thick and thin. I will choose no one over them, ever.

My phone rang, and the number was unknown, so I didn't answer. My stepdaughter texted me, saying, "Mom, it's me." She called back, and I answered. She told me that she was homeless and wanted to know the conditions for her to return home. "Conditions?" I asked. "My views haven't changed," I told her. "You need to respect my house and yourself. You need to be in school and get a job."

Honestly, this girl seems delusional. She refused to discuss the issue of sleeping with her sister's boyfriend, which I thought was pretty inappropriate. I didn't want her in my house; I felt like she would be trouble since she had no intention of working. All she wanted to do was eat, sleep, and spend time on Facebook. I told her she could come home temporarily if she followed the rules and that she would need to find her own ride.

Three days went by, and the boyfriend she was talking about on Facebook still couldn't seem to get her to my house. I went to pick her up, and my jaw dropped when I arrived. Her hair was sticking straight up, and she was wearing Daisy Dukes, a turtleneck sweater, and flip-flops. I had told her several times not to mix the seasons. Her appearance wasn't even the worst part; when she got in the car, I nearly choked from the body odor. I rolled down the windows and discreetly held my head out for some relief.

When we got to my house, she showered, and I told her she could sleep in my son's room while she was there, as I didn't expect him home until the beginning of the following year. I wanted to give her some time to relax, so I decided to have a sit-down with her in a day or so.

PAPER CHASE

The next morning, I woke her up and told her we needed to talk. First, I emphasized that I loved her. I explained that she needed to set specific short-term and long-term goals, as well as a daily plan to work toward those goals. I provided her with job search tips and recommended a community college in the area. Keith helped her get a temporary position at his brother's office so she would have some money to catch the bus. Since she had a history of wasting money, I reminded her to ensure she bought a bus pass and saved enough to get her state identification.

Two weeks passed, and the routine remained the same. I had to ask her to get off Facebook at 3 a.m. so she would have the energy to look for a job the next day. One evening, after coming home from work, I sat down at my computer for class and discovered it seemed to have a virus. It turned out that my bonus daughter had downloaded a bunch of music onto it. After four hours of repairs, I had to ask her not to touch my computer again unless she

PAPER CHASE

was completing a job application. This was turning into a nightmare.

The next morning, she claimed our dog had eaten all her money. She expected us to believe that the dog had eaten about $25 in paper money and a few coins. Who did she think we were? What 19-year-old would come up with such a ridiculous story? Besides, our puppy had trouble eating dog food, let alone money. I eventually found out that each day she left, claiming to look for work, she was actually going to fast-food restaurants to eat and then returning home.

That was the last straw; she had to go! She was up at 2 a.m., constantly updating Facebook with posts like, "Oh, how I love him." What was she thinking? She was down and out, with nothing going for herself, and her focus was on a guy? The next morning, I informed her that she would need to make alternate living arrangements. I felt that if I continued to take care of her, she wouldn't change. It was time for tough love from here on out!

PAPER CHASE

Epilogue: Triumph and Transformation

I had been driving for forty-five minutes, wondering when I would finally arrive. I was on my way to meet with my son, his counselor, and his probation officer at the boys' school. The school where my son was placed was in a rural area, and according to my GPS, I still had an hour and fifteen minutes to go. I was so excited to see him and talk to him; he hadn't been allowed any contact with the family until he proved himself, what they called "trustworthy." Now that he had demonstrated that trustworthiness, we were discussing plans for his future, including which school he would attend and his living arrangements. Given all the trouble he had been in, the probation officer wasn't sure if he could return home after his release. "Of course, he can come home," I stated confidently.

We talked for hours about my son's challenges and the best ways to help him move forward. However, I had one concern about his return, Keith. My son was unaware that Keith was

PAPER CHASE

living with me. In fact, I had kept it a secret from everyone except Aunt Latrice. Latrice gossiped a lot but was generally non-judgmental. I guess she had done enough in her past to avoid casting stones at anyone.

After our meeting, I was allowed to stay and visit with my son for a while. This was the perfect opportunity to discuss our relationship and get some things out in the open. My son apologized for stealing from me and promised to pay me back for everything. As I looked into his eyes, I held back tears. I expressed to him my worries during his absence, sharing my worst fear—that he might end up dead or in prison. I reassured him, "You don't owe me anything. I just want you to focus on staying off drugs and making better decisions."

We hugged, and I said, "Son, I have to tell you something." He looked at me with concern and fell silent. I had been dreading this conversation because I didn't want it to set back his recovery. I explained that Keith had been living with me and

PAPER CHASE

shared my concerns about how my son would feel about it.

My son responded in a way I didn't expect. He said, "You know what, Mom? I want whatever will make you happy. But if he disrespects you while I'm there, I will have to talk to him." He reassured me that he no longer held grudges against Keith but wouldn't tolerate any disrespect toward me. I assured him that there would be no physical violence because Keith wasn't physically threatening anymore. What I really wanted to say was that Keith was so sick that if he even tried to hit me, it would be the last thing he ever did.

We talked and reminisced for a little longer before saying our goodbyes. The plan was for him to come home on a pass for Christmas, so we were both excited about the visit.

On my way home, I reflected on my life, recalling it like scenes from a movie. My first memory is of Big Momma's voice, and I remember how much of my childhood was filled with fear. I

PAPER CHASE

thought about the high expectations she had for me and the accomplishments I managed to achieve. Tears streamed down my face like a river as I realized my life was far from what I wanted or dreamed it would be—my version of "success."

At home, I faced my ex-husband, whom I despised. His kiss felt like a slimy serpent crawling on my skin. Each night was a struggle as he invaded my space. The night before had been particularly hard; he entered my room uninvited, like a monster. I shouted, "I'm not a kid! **NO MEANS NO!** I told you I don't want to have sex with you, Keith!" He hurled every derogatory name at me that he could think of. I was too exhausted to argue; I had been up all night studying for midterms.

After our argument, he insisted on sleeping in my bed, claiming it was "more comfortable" and that his back hurt. I said, "Keith, don't touch me; just go to sleep, okay?"

PAPER CHASE

A few hours later, I was jolted awake by Keith's loud screams. He yelled, "Something got me, something got me!" I quickly turned on the light and saw a large, frightening scorpion in the bed with us. It had stung Keith on his face and hand. I immediately Googled what to do for a scorpion sting, gave him a cold compress, and instructed him to wash the affected areas with soap and water. Meanwhile, a part of me thought, "That's what you get!"

Who was I fooling? This couldn't continue, and I didn't want to jeopardize my soul by wishing harm on someone or hurting him. Once he gathered his wits from the sting of our argument, he accused me of putting the Scorpion on him. I just looked at him with a blank expression and didn't respond. I felt miserable being around Keith; he seemed to be sucking the life out of me. My life was far from enjoyable. Even though each day was a blessing, each morning was dreadful because I knew I would either have to fight him off or look at him.

PAPER CHASE

I asked him several times to leave me alone or sleep in my son's bed. We never went anywhere together because, honestly, I didn't want to be seen with him after he had been frolicking around town with a woman he always referred to as a friend. More than not wanting to be seen with him, I was embarrassed for myself. Regardless of the bind I was in or what we needed, I wondered how I could have sunk so low. What's even sadder is that he thinks he loves me, which couldn't be further from the truth. I believe he loved the idea of not being alone. Each day, I told myself it would be easier if he would just expire—yes, die. That's not right. How would his family feel? How would the kids feel? Would I feel guilty about it forever? So, rather than continuing to jeopardize my soul, I decided to tell Keith that he must respect my space or prepare to move out immediately.

I arrived home from work one day feeling very upset; my eyes were red and swollen from crying. It had been an especially difficult week—dealing with my son's issues, my stepdaughter, and fighting off

PAPER CHASE

Keith all night. My stepdaughter had decided to go to Indiana with her biological mother's family, but not before spreading awful lies about me and trying to make me out to be the bad guy. If my stepson hadn't gone to Indiana with them, I'm sure he wouldn't be in prison now.

I was really worried about my future. When would I start living and be truly happy? Regardless of my idea of success—stability, loyalty, independence—nothing is more valuable than being genuinely loved. I had so much on my mind and decided it was time for a drastic change. I was more determined than ever to change my circumstances. I walked into the house and yelled, "Hello!" in my Madea voice, as I usually did. I asked my youngest daughter where her dad was. Before she could answer, my 15-year-old came out of her room and said, "Mom, I need to talk to you."

"Mom, you won't believe what happened!" Joy yelled in excitement, obviously happy and jumping up and down. "My sister is getting married! My sister is getting married!" she exclaimed. "Yeah,

PAPER CHASE

Mom, he bought her a ring and everything!" Joy explained. I stood there, silent, feeling like everything was about to change in my oldest daughter's life. She didn't see what I saw—by now, I knew the signs. My first emotion was a draining feeling, similar to what I felt when I was near Keith. As I stared into emptiness, I thought, How can I save my daughter? I walked into my room and realized that every trace of Keith was gone. Finally, I thought he had decided to move on. I asked the girls if they had seen him, and they said he was gone when they got home.

I am running a few minutes late; my previous meeting is running over.

PAPER CHASE

Resources For Healing

The situation made me reflect on how I felt when my entire family stopped speaking to me, and I knew I would never do that to my own daughter. I wanted to be supportive of her choices, but I was determined to share the harsh realities, no matter what. You see, if a relationship causes you to lose yourself, your identity, and your peace of mind, it is not worth the time and effort—regardless of how much you think you love them or how much they claim to love you.

I had a long conversation with my daughter about the warning signs of a controlling and abusive person. But did she listen? Of course not! We talked about the situations the children had witnessed me endure and how those situations made them feel. She admitted that their childhood was traumatic because of living with an abusive person, yet she did not recognize the same risks in her own life. I couldn't be angry, though, because I, too, had been in denial.

PAPER CHASE

I thought about how I could help my daughter, so I requested to meet with her fiancé and his mother. What a circus that was! Some people are in complete denial. Naturally, the mother put on a show, acting as if her son was an angel. Eventually, I grew tired of the charades and spoke bluntly. I said, "Mark, if you ever put your hands on my daughter, I will be on your case like white on rice." He looked at me like a deer in headlights and simply said, "Okay." In my mind, I thought he better believe me—I would do anything to protect my family.

I called Stephanie and told her we were going to plan a wedding. With the help of my sister, Agelique, and me, we funded and organized the wedding and reception. Stephanie wanted to get married on Valentine's Day on South Mountain, with the reception the following Saturday. The wedding was beautiful, and the best part was that the preparations gave my daughters and me some

PAPER CHASE

much-needed bonding time with Stephanie and her daughters.

As we celebrated, I couldn't help but sing along with LL Cool J: "We're going back to Cali... Cali... Cali... Humph, I don't think so." I thought, man, we need a vacation after this wedding! I called Stephanie and asked if she was interested in a family trip to LA, where we could take the kids shopping in the Garment District. I only had my two youngest daughters and my son living at home with me; the older children were on their own.

Stephanie had always struggled with her menstrual cycle, and she had recently lost a lot of weight due to endometriosis. She told me she was going to have a hysterectomy because it would resolve her issues. I found it concerning that someone as young as Stephanie—only 32—would need such a procedure. So, I suggested we have a girls' day to discuss it further.

PAPER CHASE

At the nail shop, I asked the small Vietnamese woman to make my water as hot as possible. "I love pedicures!" Stephanie said excitedly. "Girl, you know I'll be needing a cigarette after mine," I joked, and we both laughed. This was one of our usual activities together; we often enjoyed a little drink from her flask and relaxed in the massage chairs in silence.

Stephanie then looked at me and asked, "What are you going to do about my nephew?" I stared at her in confusion because I had no idea what she was talking about. She explained that he had been using drugs—hard drugs, not just weed. I was shocked; that explained a lot about his behavior. Stephanie went on to say that having good fathers missing in the home significantly impacts children's development. She was sharing so much insight; you would have thought Maya Angelou had personally taught her.

PAPER CHASE

Stephanie also revealed that her husband had been having affairs and that she had found condoms in their vehicle. She suspected he was seeing multiple people while working his graveyard shift.

She expressed that her children were unappreciative, disrespectful, and lazy. "You know what, sis? After my surgery, I'm going to move into an apartment on my own. I won't stick around much longer to be mistreated by everyone in my house."

After our pedicures, we went to lunch and talked for hours about our childhoods and the traumatic experiences of sexual and physical abuse. We laughed about the good times and our childhood fights over our "wanna-be gangbanger activities." It was a wonderful day, I thought, as we pulled up to her house and I fished for my keys. Just as I was getting out of the car, she said, "Sis, do you have any money?" I replied, "Of course I do!" She explained that she needed $1,500 to cover the deductible for her procedure, and I agreed to lend it to her.

PAPER CHASE

I called Stephanie to let her know we were about to get on the highway and asked her if she wanted to meet me on the Southside. Stephanie was visiting my mother, who lived near a freeway exit where we could meet up. When we pulled up to the car, my sister was absolutely glowing. I asked her, "Why do you look so pretty today?" She looked at me as if she didn't realize she was looking extra cute. "Okay... Sis, I see you," I said, smiling. Just then, she lifted her flask to take a drink. I exclaimed, "Sis, it's 8 AM! What the hell are you doing drinking this early?" After scolding her for not only drinking early but also for drinking while driving, we hugged each other tightly and got back on the I-10 headed for California.

I had never walked so much in my life; we must have returned to the car twenty times to drop off our shopping bags. We visited Beverly Hills, Sunset Boulevard, the beach, and the fish market on Crenshaw in Inglewood. We had a great time, and the kids shopped until they dropped—literally. The best part was that the kids were always so grateful

PAPER CHASE

for anything I did for them. "Thank you so much, Mom!" they shouted in unison. This was a major milestone for us: I showed the kids that I don't need a man to be successful, and neither do they.

It was Easter Sunday 2011. "Jesus has risen!" Stephanie shouted as we walked in, tired and worn out from our drive back from California. This was just what we needed. She had cooked as if it were Thanksgiving. Our family hadn't been close for years, but this time, some of our cousins came through, and my mother was there as well to celebrate Easter together. We all complimented Stephanie on how delicious the food was. We had the best time and decided to show the kids some of our skills. They had a recording studio in their home because my brother-in-law was into producing music. We got on the mic and even had my mom in the booth rapping.

Before we left Stephanie's house, she reminded me of the time for her surgery the following morning. We all hugged, kissed, and said our goodbyes before leaving for home.

PAPER CHASE

I thought, "What a vacation," as I lay there trying to recuperate from that shopping trip. The kids were at school, and I had one more day of vacation left. Around 11 AM, I heard Stephanie call my name, "Sheila!" as if she were lying next to me. I sat up on the side of my bed just as my phone rang. It was my brother-in-law who told me to get to the hospital because my sister was asking for me. I thought a hysterectomy wasn't life-threatening, but nonetheless, I quickly headed for the hospital. I lived in a rural area, so the drive to the hospital took about 45 minutes. I started praying while I was driving because hearing my sister call me while I was asleep felt very strange. My cell rang again, and it was my brother-in-law. He said, "Are you sitting down?" I replied, "No, I'm driving!" He told me, "She is gone, Stacey."

What?! I temporarily lost control of my vehicle, avoided an accident, and then pulled myself together. Once I arrived at the hospital, I jumped out at valet and ran up to my sister's room. I knew the room number because she had texted me that morning letting me know. I entered the room in disbelief and paused before approaching. I saw her lying there, and she just looked asleep. As I reached her body and realized that it was true—my sister had died—rage rose up in me and I began to yell, "What happened? What happened?" I started asking her to wake up while kissing and hugging her, tears rolling down my face. "No God!" I screamed. Her body was cold and still.

The doctors said that my sister died from a blood clot that formed during surgery. I was filled with rage; how could she go in for a non-life-threatening procedure and end up dying? Then I realized that my mom and my sister's children hadn't been notified yet. I took a deep breath to calm myself down and left the hospital. When I reached the valet, I was confused about how to retrieve my car since I hadn't taken a valet ticket upon arrival. After figuring out which car was mine, I headed to my mom's house.

I called her and said, "Hey, Mom, I'm on my way to get you. I need you to come to the hospital."

PAPER CHASE

My mom hesitantly agreed and came outside when I arrived. She sensed something was wrong, but I knew she wouldn't expect the news I had for her.

About fifteen minutes later, we pulled back up to the hospital, and as we got out of the car, one of the attendants asked if I would be okay. My mom looked at me and let out a scream that reminded me of the one I heard when my Big Momma passed away. A nurse rushed over with a wheelchair, and I tried to comfort my mother. She asked me, "Is my baby gone?" All I could do was shake my head, unable to speak.

Once we got to where my sister's body was, my mother went in alone. The sound of her crying was indescribable, filled with pure agony. Another trip to Timbuktu! My sister had worked in hospice for years and had burial insurance; however, some of the money was required upfront because the cemetery only accepted cash. We needed $6,800 to bury her at the same cemetery where all our family members were laid to rest.

PAPER CHASE

I took care of all the arrangements: the obituary, food and supplies, clothes for the children, and I also paid two months' worth of bills at my sister's house. I remember thinking that I would never heal from this loss and that my heart would love her forever.

"Hey, Auntie," Stephanie, my sister's oldest daughter, said. "Hey, Sugar Pie," I replied. "What's up? Why was the phone off? We've been calling nonstop." The house was a mess; things were scattered everywhere, and my nephew was walking around wearing one of my sister's blouses. "What is going on? Where is your dad?" I asked. At that moment, the lights went out. I took two deep breaths and told the kids to grab some clothes and get in the truck.

Two weeks later, we finally heard from my brother-in-law, who claimed to be away pursuing his "rap career" and dared to demand that I return the kids. When we drove back to my sister's house, we noticed a paper taped to the door. It was an eviction

PAPER CHASE

notice stating that the property needed to be vacated by the following day.

Sitting in the Social Security Administration office, I felt violated. The security guard practically frisked me because I had a bottle opener on my keychain. "Ms. Harris," a woman yelled from behind the door. I was there to help my niece apply for my sister's death benefits from Social Security for her two younger children, who were 15 and 17.

It took hours, and the longer I sat there, the angrier I became. My sister's husband had received $200,000 from the life insurance policy and then abandoned his family. After two weeks, my niece received a large lump sum. I helped my mother find a larger apartment, and the kids moved in with her. I encouraged my niece to take financial management classes and open savings accounts for the children. But not even two weeks later, she was missing in action, along with my mom's Cadillac. To make matters worse, there was no food in the house, and the cable had been shut off. "Lord God, help me not to beat the crap out of her," I said out loud. This

PAPER CHASE

situation reminded me of so many past events. Why do certain families continue to face the same issues over and over again?

My mom had been diagnosed with Parkinson's disease shortly after my sister passed away. "I'm on my way to meet with you and James," I said as I merged onto I-10. When I arrived, my mom's car was gone, and the two younger children were present but did not come out of their rooms. My mom had called me the night before, frightened and upset about a house guest she didn't even know she had. You won't believe it—my 18-year-old nephew had moved his boyfriend in. Yes, boyfriend! The police had been called multiple times over the month for various incidents, including fighting, loud music, parties, and theft. They had turned my mom's house, which was usually quiet and peaceful, into a "frat house."

I sat in my mom's living room and said to her, "Kids are different these days." This may not have been the best idea. These kids have taken over your home, and we need to establish rules and boundaries. Just then, my oldest niece walked in and barely said hello, as if I had done something wrong. I told myself, "Keep your cool, Stacey."

My mom then asked, "Honey, did you pick up Grandma's medicine?" My niece snapped at her like a Chihuahua, saying, "NO! I didn't have time; I'll try tomorrow," before heading to her bedroom. I asked, "What is it? I'll go grab it." She quickly listed about six different prescriptions and mentioned she hadn't had insulin for over a week. "What!" I shouted.

I walked down the hallway briskly, took a deep breath, and firmly knocked on her door. "I need to talk to you!" I said sternly. She exited the room, and before I could say a word, she informed me that it was none of my business. "No, little girl!" I retorted. "This is my momma, and you won't kill her like you killed yours."

As the insults flew back and forth, my mom's husband threatened to call the police. "I'm going to leave," I told my niece, "but the next time I come back, you need a plan to move yourself and your

PAPER CHASE

sister and brother out of here. You're not going to kill my momma!" I yelled as I slammed the door behind me.

After a couple of days, I called my mom to discuss the situation. She told me, "I want them to leave, but they won't. Their names are on the lease, too." I reported the situation as elder abuse and spoke with the apartment management about everything happening in the apartment. The house guest was still living there, despite my mother having asked him not to return. The apartment manager requested that I come into the office, and together we would call the police and go over to my mother's apartment to ask the house guest to leave. However, we learned they could not ask the children to leave; they would need to depart voluntarily since they were on the lease.

We waited for two hours for the police to arrive. I thought to myself, "I guess I'm going to have to stab someone to get their attention." Honestly, for preventive situations, the police aren't as quick to respond, and if you're in the wrong neighborhood, you can pretty much double the response time.

Once we arrived at my mom's apartment, just as we expected, they were inside along with the house guest. The police advised the man, who turned out to be a transient that my nephew had met months earlier, that he was trespassing. At that point, the kids scattered like cockroaches, and I asked the police to check the apartment to ensure everyone was safe. They discovered a large garbage bag filled with liquor, marijuana, prescription antidepressants, and filth in the kids' rooms.

One thing about my mom was that she enjoyed a peaceful, neat life. She was particular about cleanliness and did not invite strangers into her home. I prayed that my involvement would prompt a change and ultimately help them realize they needed their own apartment if they could not be respectful. Unfortunately, my mom was not exactly receptive to that idea. She explained that she wanted to let the kids have their way to help them through their grief. "What!" I exclaimed in anger. "My sister would have killed one of them for mistreating you!"

Several months passed, and I grew tired of the constant drama. For my sanity, I didn't speak to my mom for months, but I would hear from my children about what was happening. During this time in my life, I reflected on more pain and chaos than joy. I cried myself to sleep at night because I felt lonely and yearned for companionship – a good man.

When we are strong, we must figure out how to cope with issues that not only resolve them but also help us learn from our mistakes and break unhealthy cycles. These cycles are the chains my Big Momma would pray about. I decided to seek God and commit to being celibate–yes, celibate, no sex! I figured that since I wanted something from God, I needed to sacrifice something for Him. I had been running into the worst guys – broke, womanizers, liars, and cheaters. Honestly, I wouldn't have dared to introduce any of them to my children after what they had already experienced.

PAPER CHASE

One day during Bible study, I met Vicky, the first Black girl I had encountered who sounded like a typical Valley Girl from California. "Oh, my God!" she exclaimed. "Your skin is so pretty!" "Thank you," I replied, "your hair is pretty too!" I complimented her on the gorgeous wig she was wearing.

As time went on, we worked out every Wednesday after Bible study and became friends. Vicky was not the type of person I would usually hang out with; she was wild and often seemed to be two cards short of a full deck. The things she said made me think she was from another planet some days. My goal was to turn over a new leaf and allow a new friend into my life, aside from Agelique and Tiffany. So, I accepted Vicky for who she was, but I only hung out with her at church or to exercise.

"Hey, auntie," I said as I answered my phone. "You know your mama is in the hospital," Latrice informed me. "What?" I exclaimed, standing up from the table where I had been sitting. Latrice had called me several times earlier that day, but I answered this time because I was on my lunch break. My mom hadn't wanted me to know that she had been without her insulin for a week and had also been pushed down by my oldest niece, resulting in her hospitalization. "You're going to let them kill your mama?" she asked me. I ignored her because I knew I was doing everything I could while trying to remain peaceful. "I'll let you know how everything goes, Auntie. I'll talk to you later," I said before hanging up. I informed my supervisor that I would be leaving early for the day and headed to the hospital.

Despite my best efforts to stay calm, by the time I arrived at the hospital, I felt like I was erupting like a volcano. I was overwhelmed with emotions because I believed that if the situation continued, I would end up burying my mother. Additionally, I could see that the behavior of the kids was escalating, and I feared they would hurt someone else.

PAPER CHASE

As I stepped onto the elevator, my phone rang. It was my oldest daughter. I answered, "Hey, sweetie." "Hi, Mom," she responded cheerfully. "We went to Grandma's to bring her a gift, but she didn't answer, so we let ourselves in with your key." I had given her the key earlier so she could check on my mom when I wasn't available.

Suddenly, I heard a voice scream in the background. My daughter then yelled, "No! No! No! I'M PREGNANT! I'M PREGNANT!" Then I heard two gunshots followed by silence. In an instant, I turned and ran like a track star toward my car in the hospital parking lot. Just then, my daughter called me back, hysterical. She said, "They jumped me! They jumped me!"

She explained that when she entered my mom's house, all three of my sister's children had attacked her, and my mother's husband had fired two warning shots to stop them from injuring her.

PAPER CHASE

What in the world just happened? I asked myself as I shook my head in disbelief, listening to Mary J. Blige's song "My Life" in the background; her music can really make you think. Within two weeks, I moved my mother out of that apartment and into a retirement community where she could enjoy bingo and learn Zumba. The previous apartment management had to force the children to move out, and that was that!

To this day, I have not spoken to those kids. I've heard they are still causing drama wherever they go and have reconnected with their father. It's not that I hold a grudge; it's just that I have no time for foolishness. We can love someone from a distance, and that's how it will have to be between my nieces, nephews, and me.

What do you do when you struggle to understand how to love yourself, let alone someone else? Often, the root of the issue is a lack of self-love, whether due to past traumas, the absence of parental figures, or negative examples from those around us. Regardless of the cause, finding love is essential for our lives. I've explored various self-help books that emphasize "dating yourself." The concept is simple: when you treat yourself well, you won't allow others to mistreat you. I even created a list detailing the qualities I desire in a husband, complete with a checklist of questions to ask at certain times. Each morning, I pray for the husband I have yet to meet: "Lord, protect him and his wisdom from the crown of his head to the soles of his feet; keep him safe and prosper him, Lord, in the name of Jesus." A vital lesson I've learned is to pace myself, as people can change, especially after intimacy. My list is titled "I am who God created me to be." I encourage you to craft your list, starting with who you believe God designed you to be. Reflect on your soul and identify the desires of your heart. Are you experiencing those desires? This is where breaking old chains begins! Dismantle every negative assertion ever made against you, even those you've told yourself. Remember, you can achieve anything you set your mind to. Let's not over spiritualize this; mistakes stem from our foolishness at times. Nurturing a closer relationship

PAPER CHASE

with God regarding my purpose has fueled my determination to succeed in the right way.

PAPER CHASE

Questions For Reflection

I am who God created me to be, and I will fulfill His purpose for my life. I embrace my uniqueness in all that I am and do. I refuse to settle for anything less than God's best for me. I am beautiful, intelligent, resourceful, and fun. I take pride in myself and care for my health. God has designed a husband who will love me.

Here are some questions to consider:

Does he possess qualities that I value?

Does he make me feel good?

Does he treat me the way I want to be treated?

What is his relationship with his family and parents?

Does he have children, and more? importantly, is he present and provides for them?

Does he value his health?

Does he value cleanliness?

Any baby mamma drama?

PAPER CHASE

Other Conversation Starters

1. What is your profession?

2. Where are you from?

3. What is the one thing about yourself that you would like me to know?

4. When was your last relationship, and how long did it last?

5. What are you looking for in a relationship?

6. What do you think is the most critical value in a relationship?

7. Do you want to marry, or have you ever been married?

8. What are the most essential qualities in a mate?

9. Do you want/do you have any children?

10. What do you do for fun?

11. What are you most proud of?

12. Is religion important to you?

PAPER CHASE

13. Do you follow politics? Are you a Democrat or a Republican?

14. What is your most treasured possession and why?

15. What is your favorite month of the year and why?

16. Which is your favorite book/movie?

17. Which is the last book/movie you read?

18. Which is the one job in the world that you would love to do?

19. What is your favorite music and your favorite singer/band?

20. Do you like animals/keep pets?

21. How do you spend your spare time?

22. Where do you see yourself in five years?

23. If you were an animal in the wild, what would you be?

24. Do you believe a cup is half empty or half full?

25. If you could travel back through time, what single mistake would you correct in life?

26. Is sexual compatibility important to you?

27. Which was the first crush you ever had?

28. What makes you laugh/cry?

29. If you have friends coming over, what would you cook?

30. Describe your perfect holiday.

31. What is the last CD you bought?

32. Are you a morning person or a night person?

33. Who is your favorite actor/actress/celebrity and why?

34. Who is your favorite sports person?

PAPER CHASE

35. What is your favorite sporting activity?

36. Which is your favorite genre of movies - comedy/thriller/action?

PAPER CHASE

Where Are They Now

Keith ultimately returned to his hometown in Illinois, and what I've heard from mutual acquaintances is far from reassuring. They say he's using cocaine at an alarming rate and is frequently drowning his sorrows in clubs, drinking, and partying nonstop. Can you believe he was high the entire time we were married, and I never even suspected it? It all makes sense now—his explosive violence was often triggered in an instant. There are even whispers that he may have more children on the way—same old Keith. I've heard he's battling his usual health issues, like high blood pressure and diabetes, yet somehow finds the energy to hit on women.

As for Aunt June, she remains ever the same. To this day, she's in and out of prison, chasing whatever drugs she can get her hands on. She even brought another child into the world, but fortunately, that child is being cared for by the father's family. She shockingly confessed to having a brief affair with Keith—what a twisted connection! I've tried to help her; I ventured down to "Hoe Stroll" on Van Buren, notorious for its drugs and prostitution, to pick her up several times and persuade her to go to rehab. Yet, every time she'd come down from her high, she'd vanish back to the streets.

Sadly, Keith Jr. has continued the cycle, committing a violent crime in Indiana and receiving a twenty-year prison sentence. I reach out to him every so often, but it's emotionally draining and brings back waves of painful memories. His struggles with the law seem endless, and I'm heartbroken to know he's still grappling with meth binges. Every night, I pray for his healing and beg for God's protection over him.

I lift my youngest son in my prayers, as he battles addiction and mental health

PAPER CHASE

challenges that mirror those faced by my grandfather. There is a palpable distance between us, and he carries a deep resentment toward me rooted in his difficult childhood experiences.

"Hey baby," I said, smiling as I answered the phone. "Hey boo," Reggie replied. You might be wondering who Reggie is, so let me rewind and catch you up on the story.

Vicky told me about her cousin Reggie one day while I was venting about my fear of dating again. She explained that he was a lovely, employed single father who had been in an abusive relationship. The woman he was with liked to fight, but he never retaliated. Unfortunately, she didn't respect him and ended up cheating on him. Vicky described how kind he was and how he always helped the female cousins by fixing things around their homes. I expressed my surprise, saying, "Vicky, we've known each other for three years, and you never mentioned that you have family here! I thought they were all in California." I was a little annoyed, but she explained that she assumed I was always busy, so she never brought it up.

Interestingly, when she told me about Reggie, I never asked how he looked. Vicky said she would give him my number, and I tried not to get too excited. A week passed, and I received a call from an unknown number. I answered in the middle of catering, saying, "Hello..." loudly because I was in a rush.

"Hi," the voice on the other end responded. "Is this Stacey?" I immediately said, "Hi Reggie!" Somehow, I just knew it was him. We connected right away. I signaled for one of my staff members to take over in the kitchen and stepped into a back room. We talked and laughed as if we had known each other for years. It turned out that the location where I was catering was right around the corner from where he lived. A lump formed in my throat as we both realized it. After what felt like an hour of silence, I broke the quiet by saying, "So, are you coming?" He replied, "I'm putting on my shoes." I had to giggle under my breath; it was like we were sharing thoughts.

About twenty minutes later, I looked out the window and saw the truck he had described pulling into the large parking lot. It was a windy day, and I was wearing a cute little romper with an apron over it. The wind blew my short, honey-colored hair, brushing it gently against my rosy cheeks. I had just refreshed my bronze-colored lip gloss, which contrasted nicely with the gold tones in my skin. As I walked outside, I saw him exiting the truck, and nothing could have prepared me for what was about to happen.

Picture the most stunning man you've ever encountered—so captivating that it makes you question your very thoughts. He embodies every quality you've ever desired and shares your dreams. Now, imagine that he will love you unconditionally for the rest of your lives. In that moment, I realized he was the husband I had always envisioned and fervently prayed for each morning. As butterflies danced in my stomach and my head spun with excitement, we embraced in a heartfelt hug. This man towered over 6 feet tall, boasting a physique that was nothing short of perfection. His skin radiated the warmth of caramel, and his smile infused my heart with energy, while his scent enveloped me like a field of lilacs. He was a divine blend of the suave Denzel Washington and the rugged allure of The Game. "I hear you, Lord!" I whispered to myself, feeling a swoon of happiness.

Guess who discovered real love for the first time? This journey has led me to the kindest, most genuine man I have ever known. He accepts me for who I am—my good, my bad, and yes, even my ugly. He cares for my children and embraces them as his own, all while upholding the old-school values of hard work and monogamy that are so important to me. His name is Reggie, and you know what? I absolutely deserve this!

Falling for someone whose inner beauty shines brighter than any superficial "Paper Chase" has been transformative. Reflecting on my path, I recognize that it was my willingness to embrace differences that brought me to my husband. Without my friendship with Vicky, we might never have met. It feels as though all those prayers I've whispered over the years are finally being answered.

Loving myself has opened the door to accepting God's best for me and has enabled me to love another wholeheartedly. I am truly blessed! My husband is my knight in shining armor, embodying every single item on my "wish list." This experience reminds me that love is possible when we open our hearts and remain true to ourselves. He cherishes my children as if they were his own, and he stands by me as my friend, protector, passionate lover, and the finest example of a father and man I have ever known.

As I gaze at our wedding picture with joy, admiration, and commitment, I can't help but think, "I never want to wake from this dream." If God can forgive my past, guide me through my mistakes, protect me, and heal my broken heart, then He can do the same for you. I am finally HAPPY!

PAPER CHASE

My marriage and relationship are now an example that will cause a generational shift. My daughters and I have had countless conversations about making wiser choices than I did and about the importance of loving ourselves first. My three oldest have all excelled in life—attending college, landing jobs, and starting families. Lil' Mamma, ever practical, has declared she won't have children, focusing instead on her travels and finances. The youngest two still live with me, and I thank God they've been able to witness my new marriage and the love of my husband. They observe how he treats me and takes care of our family, setting a standard for the kind of husband they should aspire to find. Despite their young age, they see the transformative difference in our lives, and thanks to my marriage, they know they won't settle for anything less than the best.

My mother has made significant improvements in her health. She has developed a social life and participates in Zumba classes, as

PAPER CHASE

well as various weekly events at her senior living facility.

Unfortunately, I have not heard from my nieces or my nephew since then. It's as if they vanished completely; there hasn't been a single rumor or update about them.

Now, it's time for the next chapter of my life because I'm still grinding...

PAPER CHASE

Luke 12:48 Easy-to-Read Version (ERV)

⁴⁸ But what about the servant who does not know what his master wants? He also does things that deserve punishment. But he will get less punishment than the servant who knew what he should do. Whoever has been given much will be responsible for much. Much more will be expected from the one who has been given more."

PAPER CHASE

ABOUT THE AUTHOR

Introducing Sheila "Honey" Reed, a dedicated Licensed Associate Addiction Counselor (LAAC) whose passion for mental health care and community counseling has shaped her remarkable journey. With a wealth of certifications in trauma, crisis intervention, and infant mental health clinical practice, Honey exemplifies a commitment to holistic care that goes beyond traditional methods.

Since 2015, she has made impactful contributions in the fields of Mental Health and

PAPER CHASE

Addiction Treatment, as well as Early Childhood Education. Her approach leverages evidence-based practices to ensure that clients not only address their mental health needs but also nurture their emotional, physical, and social well-being.

Honey actively engages in community service initiatives focused on suicide prevention and addiction treatment, using her expertise to educate and support individuals and families alike. Through professional development workshops, she empowers educators to provide culturally responsive and positive learning experiences in early childhood settings.

As a trainer, she teaches resilience-building techniques to caregivers, offering them the tools needed to support children who have experienced trauma. Honey's ultimate goal is to foster nurturing environments where both children and caregivers can thrive, enhancing the overall mental health and well-being of the community.

PAPER CHASE

"Love yourself enough to make your heart happy".

-Sheila "Honey" Reed-

www.ingramcontent.com/pod-product-compliance
Lightning Source LLC
Chambersburg PA
CBHW071302110426
42743CB00042B/1148